The NPR Curious Listener's Guide to

Classical
Music

The NPR Curious Listener's Guide to

Classical
Music

TIM SMITH

A Grand Central Press Book
A Perigee Book

A Perigee Book
Published by The Berkley Publishing Group
A division of Penguin Putnam Inc.
375 Hudson Street
New York, New York 10014

Produced by Grand Central Press
Paul Fargis, Director
Judy Pray, Executive Editor
Nick Viorst, Series Editor

NATIONAL PUBLIC RADIO
Murray Horwitz, Vice-President, Cultural Programming
Andy Trudeau, Executive Producer, Cultural Programming
Benjamin Roe, Senior Producer, Special Projects, Cultural Programming
Barbara A. Vierow, Project Manager, Business Development
Kate Elliott, Project Manager, Business Development

First Perigee edition: August 2002

Visit our website at www.penguinputnam.com

Library of Congress Cataloging-in-Publication Data

Smith, Tim.
    The NPR curious listener's guide to classical music / Tim Smith.
        p.   cm.
    Includes index.
    ISBN 0-399-52795-8
    1. Music appreciation.   I. National Public Radio (U.S.)   II. Title.
MT90 .S65 2002
781.6'8—dc21
                                                      2001055162

PRINTED IN THE UNITED STATES OF AMERICA
10   9   8   7   6   5   4   3   2   1

Contents

Acknowledgments

My thanks, first of all, to the late music historian and photo archivist Otto Bettmann, who kept encouraging me to write a book; I'm sorry it took me so long to follow his advice. And thanks to my partner, Robert Leininger, for pushing me to finish the product and helping me in various ways during the process.

Another round of thanks to my editor, Nick Viorst, for his remarkable patience and good judgment. And to Michael Tilson Thomas for his invaluable foreword, not to mention the many years of inspiration his ever-curious musical mind has given me. I also greatly appreciate all the folks at NPR, especially Ben Roe, who endorsed my participation in this project.

Foreword

by Michael Tilson Thomas

NPR is one of America's greatest cultural resources. Its spirit of open-minded inquiry into the nature of things has made it an informative and entertaining part of our lives. It is the style of NPR to offer a fresh and direct approach to all the areas of its wide-ranging curiosity. It makes us aware of so many new thoughts, as well as bringing us new insights into those that are familiar.

With this guide, NPR fans will have the chance to discover refreshing new perspectives about Western civilization's most abstract and emotionally affecting art: classical music. Classical music, for one thousand years, has expressed man's most personal thoughts about God, life, love, despair, fantasy, rage, resignation, and joy—the whole gamut of what it means to be alive.

There's no other music that has the range and diversity of classical music. Its rich tradition can be an intricate tangle of styles, forms, composers, artists, and aesthetic movements. Yet at all times it has sung and witnessed profoundly and directly the beautiful bittersweetness of being.

This guide, written by the enthusiastically witty and knowledgeable Tim Smith, offers the reader insights into classical music's mysteries, while at the same time clarifying its central sincere purpose of communication and expression. I think you'll find it a welcome addition to your library.

Michael Tilson Thomas assumed his post as the San Francisco Symphony's eleventh music director in September 1995, consolidating a strong relationship with the Orchestra that began with his debut there in 1974 at the age of twenty-nine. Along with his post in San Francisco, Michael Tilson Thomas serves as artistic director of the New World Symphony, a national training orchestra for the most gifted graduates of America's conservatories, which he founded in 1988, and as principal guest conductor of the London Symphony Orchestra, where he served as principal conductor for seven years.

Introduction

Classical music is a source of inspiration, exhilaration, and comfort to some people. To others, it's an intimidating mystery, or maybe even an extreme annoyance.

Not long ago, a story appeared about how West Palm Beach police started piping in the greatest hits of Bach, Mozart, and Beethoven twenty-four hours a day from an abandoned building in a neighborhood being overrun by drug dealers. That did the trick. The place has never been safer. There have been similar reports over the years of classical music aimed at teenaged loiterers at convenience stores.

The idea that the sounds of this aural art form could drive anyone away is almost as scary as a drug-infested street corner or a bunch of kids blocking the way to a quick pick-up of milk. It is a dispiriting sign of the times that classical music does not enjoy the widespread admiration, respect, and outright love it once did, and that many young people, in particular, find it hard to take. The steady decline in music education in the schools certainly hasn't helped. The enormous allure and omnipresence of pop music, combined with a general dumbing down of culture, has also played a part.

And yet, classical music endures. Its relative lack of popularity in no way diminishes its status as an integral part of what we call civilization. As such, this music will always have its admirers, will always attract the curious of all ages (even a few rock stars interested in expanding their horizons), ethnic backgrounds, religious and political persuasions, nationalities, and orientations of one kind or another. Classical fans may not always be numerous, but they will be enthusiastic and loyal.

What makes classical music worthy of exploration, let alone devotion? What gives it such lasting power? All art forms involve some sort of qualitative evaluation. Few people would argue that the figures of clowns and Elvis painted on velvet and sold every weekend on gas station lots are equal in worth to the *Mona Lisa* or an abstract canvas by Jackson Pollack. We know instinctively that there is a difference in quality of artistry involved, even before we address the issue of price. We know instinctively why certain artwork ends up on display in museums and why crowds flock to see it.

It's much the same with music, although the differences are not always as obvious as between those velvet paintings and Rembrandts. A simple folk song, passed down through generations, is certainly art; Aaron Copland's *Appalachian Spring*, which incorporates a simple folk-hymn, is arguably a more sophisticated form of art. A well-crafted pop song by Cole Porter or George Gershwin or Elton John or Sting is certainly art, too. Yet a song by Schubert or Schumann, with words by a poet rather than a lyricist and music written for a classically trained singer, is on another artistic level—not necessarily better, but clearly aiming for something greater. Likewise, symphonies and concertos and string quartets and oratorios all strive for a high artistic ground.

Although classical music very much reflects its own time, it is simultaneously steeped in traditions that may stretch back for centuries. That's one reason it's called "classical." The neat thing about those traditions is that they have a way of speaking to Curious Listeners in a remarkably direct, inviting way. Mozart may have died in 1791, but people hearing his music for the first time in 1891 or 1991 could understand it on at least a fundamental level, could relate to it, with hardly any effort, as if it were freshly written. The melodies stick quickly in the head; the harmonies make perfect sense; the rhythms are readily discernible.

Subconsciously, at the very least, we in the Western world are connected to the roots of classical music, for they are the same roots that have produced all of Western music. Music— classical and pop—is created out of the same twelve tones of the scale that have yielded the same chords for centuries, the same twelve tones that have also produced the complicated, dissonant sounds that erupted in the twentieth century. Appreciating the common ground shared by so many types of music is one way for the Curious Listener to become comfortable with the classics.

The urge to dig into classical music can be sparked in any number of ways. Sometimes, it's nothing more than a TV commercial or movie scene with a classical composition in the background that hooks someone's interest. A chance encounter on the radio can do the same. Some people find themselves, even against their will, dragged along by a spouse or buddy to a classical concert—and end up liking what they hear. Those lucky enough to have music courses at school may discover a lot more pleasure in subsequent exposure than they had ever imagined.

Whatever the entry point, the Curious Listener will keep going and keep exploring. Learning to appreciate classical music is, like most of the finest things, a lifelong process and a lifelong delight. Folks who get hooked on the catchy rhythms and colorful sounds of Vivaldi's *The Four Seasons* may well check out works by his contemporaries of the Baroque era, Bach and Handel. Those who first come across the boldness and drama of Beethoven's Fifth Symphony may find it a natural, almost unavoidable path to his other symphonies, his concertos, and maybe piano sonatas. And from Beethoven, it can be an easy leap to Brahms, possibly even all the way to Mahler and Shostakovich.

Every Fourth of July, someone hears Tchaikovsky's *1812 Overture* for the first time and gets caught up in the exhilarating rush. (Why Americans celebrate their independence day with a composition about the Russian defeat of Napoleon's army is a subject for another book.) A logical move is to buy a recording of that stirring Tchaikovsky work, which, since it's not enough to fill an entire compact disc, means automatic exposure to other works, perhaps by Tchaikovsky or fellow Russians. And that, in turn, can lead in all sorts of directions.

It's not that you will end up loving everything you hear; most listeners develop certain limits, specific areas of attraction and of alienation. That's perfectly normal. To some, Rachmaninoff is a kind of aural sex; to others, his music is thick goo. To some, Bach is the epitome of genius and perfection; to others, he sounds mathematical. To some, Mozart is pure heaven;

to others, pure ennui. Some lucky listeners can thrive on atonality; some only writhe in agony to it. Part of the fun is trying out different composers, different styles, different sounds. Music from any time period can connect with us, can entertain, intrigue or deeply touch us. All it takes is curiosity, and the willingness to listen.

This book makes no attempt to answer all the questions about classical music, but only to provide a basic (and subjective) guide to this endlessly rewarding topic. In addition to a look at the meaning of the term *classical music*, there is a short history of the art form and a necessarily selective list of important composers, performers, and compositions. Nothing can take the place of actual listening, and nothing beats listening in person at concerts, but recordings offer an easy, and sometimes very affordable, way of increasing knowledge and intensifying interest. So you'll also find a list of suggested recordings that represent some of the best classical music, from the distant past up to the present.

Whether you decide to delve much more deeply into the subject or to maintain a casual relationship with the art form, the main thing is to get your ears wet and keep them open to the possibilities that are out there, to go a little further than just the compositions that spark the initial curiosity and pleasure, to test your own limits and tastes.

So plunge right in. The music's fine.

The NPR Curious Listener's Guide to

Classical
Music

ONE

What Is Classical Music?

It's not pop music, but it has lots of catchy tunes.

It's not rock music, but it often has a good beat and you can dance to it.

It's not folk music, but it often contains folk songs and rhythms.

It's not jazz, but some of it used to be improvised, and some of it still allows for freedom of expression. And an awful lot of it shares a defining characteristic of jazz—a democratic sense of creative community.

Classical music obviously means many things, encompasses many expressions. But for a long time now, the term has been almost universally understood to mean a type of music in the Western world that is art first, entertainment second. So there's an easy answer to the question, "What is classical music?" It's the kind that doesn't make much money.

That wasn't always the case. Time was when classical composers wrote for and were handsomely rewarded by kings and religious leaders. Today, with pop music ruling the world, classical music may have lost much of its marketability, but none of its significance.

The very word *classical* connotes something of lasting value, something conceived with certain standards in mind. This has led some people to slap an additional label onto such music—"elitist." But that's a cheap shot. There is nothing restrictive about classical music. Although it is best appreciated, most deeply understood, by those who study it in some detail, it is essentially accessible to anyone with open ears. And that act of listening is a very important part of this art form. Despite its use in shopping malls and hotel lobbies, most classical music is intended to be foreground, not background; it wants to be front and center, not piped-in.

The word *classical* conveys structural order, a clear sense of form, design, and content; this is certainly part of what makes classical music classical. It can be "seen" as well as heard—looked at as a kind of sonic edifice with a foundation, walls, stairways, and windows. The works of Joseph Haydn and Wolfgang Amadeus Mozart suggest perfectly proportioned eighteenth-century buildings; the ear can easily pick up the way phrases are balanced in pairs, like the same number of windows on the left and right sides of a house. In the late-nineteenth century, Anton Bruckner's very long symphonies confused many listeners, but underneath the music were clearly organized blocks of melodies and the mortar to hold them together.

Until the twentieth century, when composers began experimenting freely with form and design, classical music continued to follow basic rules relating to structure, not to mention harmony. There still was room for individuality (the great composers didn't follow the rules, but made the rules follow them), yet there was always a fundamental proportion and logic behind the design. Even after many of the rules were overturned by radical concepts in more recent times, composers, more often than not, still organized their thoughts in ways that produced an overall, unifying structure: a game plan. That's one reason the atonal, incredibly complex works by Arnold Schoenberg or Karlheinz Stockhausen, to name two twentieth-century Modernists, are nonetheless approachable. The sounds might be very strange, but the results are still decidedly classical in terms of organization.

Perhaps the most significant aspect of classical music is what composers do with the notes that they put into the structure at hand. Typically, the pop music composer is finished after creating a tune with chords (harmony) underneath it. By contrast, the classical composer's task is far from over with the writing of a melody or a chord or a rhythmic pattern; that's only the beginning. The classical composer is interested in developing the full potential of the melodic and harmonic ideas; this process of development fleshes out the bare bones of a musical form. This process will go on in each of the four movements of a symphony or the three of a concerto; a short, one-movement piano piece or an elaborate choral work.

Development can get very complicated and fanciful. A fugue by Johann Sebastian Bach illustrates how far this process could go, when a single melodic line, sometimes just a handful of notes, was all that the composer needed to create a brilliant work containing lots of intricate development within a coherent structure. Ludwig van Beethoven's famous Fifth Symphony provides an exceptional example of how much mileage a classical composer can get out of a few notes and a simple rhythmic patter. The opening da-da-da-DUM that everyone has heard somewhere or another appears in an incredible variety of ways throughout not only the opening movement, but the remaining three movements, like a kind of motto or a connective thread. Just as we don't always see the intricate brushwork that goes into the creation of a painting, we may not always notice how Beethoven keeps finding fresh uses for his motto or how he develops his material into a large, cohesive statement. But a lot of the enjoyment we get from that mighty symphony stems from the inventiveness behind it, the compelling development of musical ideas. It's the same with piece after piece of classical music, from a cello concerto by Antonín Dvořák to a string quartet by Maurice Ravel.

In a work like the *Variations on a Theme of Haydn* by Johannes Brahms, we can hear the composer dissect a single tune of several measures' duration, examine it from every harmonic and rhythmic angle, and put it back together. It's very close to what a jazz player does with a Standard like "Star Dust," only instead of improvisation, every note is on paper, providing that classical permanence and order. This structure of theme and variations has been in use by classical composers for centuries.

Unlike in jazz, when only one song gets worked over at a time, classical composers from the mid-eighteenth century made things a little more challenging. They created a musical form, used in the typical first movement of a symphony by Mozart or Robert Schumann, which involved submitting more than one theme to development within a single structure. The idea was to present themes that had contrasting characteristics and get them to interact with each other as the development process unfolded. By the time Bruckner and Gustav Mahler came along at the end of the nineteenth century and began writing gargantuan symphonies, with different groups of themes to be worked out in each movement, the concept of musical development was carried to new heights. The breadth and depth of that development enabled such composers to make a single movement last longer than an entire four-movement symphony by Haydn or Mozart from a century earlier.

In some types of classical music, the issue of development is not so prominent, but the qualities that make such works classical are still very much in evidence—the careful choice of notes, of melody and harmony, of a journey or an argument, and the sense of flow that will arrive at a resolution.

When the style known as "minimalism" emerged in the 1970s and '80s, using brief, melodic ideas and simple chords repeated over and over to a more or less steady beat, some people argued that it wasn't classical, but merely an extension of pop and rock styles. But the minimalists were just as interested in design and cohesiveness as earlier classical composers; they liked to develop their material very slowly, almost imperceptibly, changing a couple of notes or chords, or subtly varying the reiterative rhythm.

There's a direct counterpart to pop music in the classical song, more commonly called an "art song," which does not focus on the development of melodic material. Both the pop song and the art song tend to follow tried-and-true structural patterns. And both will be published in the same way—with a vocal line and a basic piano part written out underneath. But the pop song will rarely be sung and played exactly as written; the singer is apt to embellish that vocal line to give it a "styling," just as the accompanist will fill out the piano part to make it more interesting and personal. The performers might change the original tempo and mood completely. You won't find such extremes of approach by the performers of a song by Franz Schubert or Richard Strauss. These will be performed note for note because both the vocal and piano parts have been painstakingly written down by the composer with an ear for how each relates to the other. A wonderful example is Schubert's song "Gretchen at the Spinning Wheel." The piano becomes as important as the singer, for its rolling accompaniment pattern—like the turning of a spinning wheel—helps set the scene for the song. There is still room for interpretation in an art song, but it will be applied subtly, within the borders set up by the composer. As a rule, the words in these two types of song also help to distinguish them; the classical composer seeks out poetry to set to music, while the pop composer uses "lyrics," a more vernacular form of poetry.

It is almost always apparent what makes a composition classical. Such distinctive characteristics as thematic development or structure, sophisticated harmonic progression, instrumentation, technical requirements on the performers—all of these are a part of the picture. There is also a seriousness of purpose behind classical music, even such lighthearted fare as a waltz by Johann Strauss or a *Slavonic Dance* by Dvořák. (Some folks like to call classical music "serious music," but that term has, for good reasons, never really caught on.)

With classical music, it's not a case of what you hear is what you get. What you hear is only the beginning. Layer after layer of ideas and techniques and designs lie below the surface, helping to provide a clear sense of beginning, middle, and end. There is a powerful motive behind the notes, a desire to make a statement, to engage the ear and the mind, and maybe the heart, too.

Classical music, like all great art, is self-evident.

TWO

The Story of Classical Music

L ike the story of Western art or literature, the story of classical music is an old and ongoing one. It encompasses many chapters and many different styles and developments. Both gradual evolution and dramatic upheaval have been part of that history as composers and performers have contributed their distinctive efforts to the art form.

In general, classical music has tended to reflect the times. When public tastes craved elaborate art and architecture, the music was florid; when tastes called for simpler, symmetrical designs, music was simpler and symmetrical. When the Age of Enlightenment gave way to the Age of Revolution, music became more dramatic and emotional. The harshness of the twentieth century, with its epic wars and social clashes, yielded music that turned tradition on its head.

The history of classical music is part of the history of civilization.

From Darkness into Light

Classical music effectively starts with the Dark Ages, when the first substantial documentation can be found. Of particular importance are the chants (also called "plain chant") that were sung during church services starting around the mid-sixth century. Chants were meant to be sung in unison; only a single melodic line was involved, without harmony underneath it. This form of singing, which reached heights of expressiveness and haunting beauty with such composers as Hildegard of Bingen in the twelfth century, is called "monophonic"—one voice.

By the end of the twelfth century, a new style began to flourish; instead of one vocal line, three or four would be sounded simultaneously, each one independent, but fusing together in a satisfying manner. This more complex style is called "polyphony"—many voices. The evolution of polyphonic music was a dramatic development, helping to establish some of the rules about harmony and tonality that remain firmly entrenched in Western music to this day. There was no one source of these rules; several great musical minds contributed treatises on the musical theory, continuing a line of philosophical thought that had begun with the ancient Greeks, who considered music as much a science as an art. The concept of polyphony was closely allied to the gradual acceptance of a basic foundation for music—the twelve notes of the scale and the relationships between them. The first composers of the polyphonic style allowed for tones to be sounded together to create what our ears would consider to be dissonance, or at least a very stark, piquant form of harmony. There was no clear sense of chords as we think of them today; the vocal lines were truly independent. In time, a more systematic method of composing

Gregorian Chant

A good deal of mystery surrounds what is, in essence, the first substantial written music of the Western world that we have. Monks painstakingly copied it out by hand on often elaborately decorated parchment. Gregorian chants, with texts from the Bible and Roman Catholic services, were written with a single melodic line that would be sung in unison and in a free rhythm, without accompaniment. The name "Gregorian" refers to Pope Gregory the Great, whose reign was from 590 to 604; according to tradition, he received the notes of these chants directly from the Holy Spirit. But there is no evidence that Gregory had anything to do with chants; this style of liturgical music seems to have emerged a few centuries after his death. It was only in recent times that Gregorian chant emerged from its original ecclesiastical setting to become more widely appreciated. There were even a few best-selling recordings toward the end of the twentieth century that reflected the new interest in this haunting music, with its long, winding melodies and strong spiritual vibes.

emerged, and with it came a stronger sense of harmony that avoided harshness. Among the greatest exponents of this new, more refined polyphonic style, which spread throughout Europe, was Guillaume de Machaut, who is credited with composing the first complete musical setting of texts from the Roman Catholic Mass in 1370—the *Messe de Notre Dame*.

During the Middle Ages, church music—commonly called sacred music—was the primary focus of composers, and it was, by decree from Rome, unaccompanied (except, after a while, by the organ). Secular music, which could use the growing number of instruments that were emerging in Europe, was largely an extension of folk music and folk dances. One of the fascinating developments that occurred during these early days of music history was the fusion between religious and secular music. Several composers, notably Guillaume Dufay in the fifteenth century, based the melodies of their Masses on popular songs of the day, providing a strong connection for the congregation. This practice was widely imitated.

During the Renaissance, formal musical training advanced considerably. The technology of putting music onto paper also advanced thanks to the invention of music publishing in 1501; it would remain a primitive process for a long time, but it helped to spread music and the reputations of composers. There also were increased opportunities for composers and/or performers to make a living, for the church was no longer the only place where music thrived. The royal and aristocratic classes became increasingly interested in having court composers and instrumental ensembles, hired to provide fresh music on demand, and in building private theaters, where music could be performed for select audiences.

The eras prior to the Renaissance saw steady development of musical concepts and forms (all of the material from these distant centuries is often categorized as "early music"). But things really took off creatively as the Renaissance blossomed across Europe, when there was an extraordinary flourishing of music, as with all the other arts. Among the most celebrated and influential composers of the fifteenth and sixteenth centuries were Josquin Desprez and Palestrina (widely known by his surname alone), who created works equal in color and texture to the paintings of Michelangelo and Raphael. By the end of the Renaissance period, music reached new heights of complexity, far removed from the straightforward days of chant. Compositions

Musical Servants

From the Renaissance days until the late-eighteenth century, musicians found work in churches and aristocratic households and were essentially considered domestic servants. This was particularly rough on composers, who had to create new works on a regular basis (nearly every Sunday for those affiliated with churches). Just how unpleasant the life of an indentured musician could be is illustrated by a look at Johann Sebastian Bach's career. In 1717, when he tried to leave a job as court composer to the duke of Weimar, he was put in jail. Years later, when he was able to get a job at a school in Leipzig, his duties included not only teaching five dozen students and composing a great deal of music, but also performing such demeaning chores as collecting firewood.

Joseph Haydn likewise spent about thirty years in the eighteenth century shackled to an employer, primarily Prince Nikolaus Esterhazy of the Hungarian royalty. The steady work and decent pay certainly proved beneficial, but Haydn had to wear a servant's uniform and compose anything his master desired, including music for mechanical clocks. Only after the prince's death did Haydn get to enjoy the kind of life a great composer deserves.

grew longer as well as more difficult, with richer harmonies and more elaborate melodies; instrumental ensembles likewise expanded. All of this expansion, this burst of expressive power, set the stage for the next great era of music history.

Baroque Beauty

The complicated polyphonic style developed during the Renaissance segued neatly into the Baroque era—roughly from around the start of the seventeenth century to the middle of the eighteenth. It was during this period that many of the foundations of Western classical music were firmly put in place. Gradually, all of the ideas about melody and harmony that had been tried out during previous times crystallized into standard rules of composition. As before, there were many individuals involved in the development of this musical theory; some of them were composers, like Claudio Monteverdi and Jean-Philippe Rameau, whose brilliant works helped to establish ideals of harmonic logic, melodic expressiveness, and rhythmic vitality. Out of the advanced thinking about music came the refinement of an element that had begun to assert itself in polyphonic music of the Renaissance period: imitation, a method of having an independent line in a piece of music imitate, a few moments later, the melody of a previous line. The Baroque composers relished the possibilities in this imitative style of polyphony, which came to be called "counterpoint." Johann Sebastian Bach and Antonio Vivaldi were among the masters of this musical language, which had as its main characteristic a constant motion of melody and rhythm, a sense of ideas in flux, yet somehow fusing together into a tight, cohesive thought. Learning how to speak this musical language required enormous technical and artistic skill on the part of players.

The most elevated form of counterpoint is the fugue, a kind of complex musical argument worked out and brought to a clear resolution by multiple "voices." Several other clear-cut musical forms evolved, most of them based on the rhythms and moods of old dance forms—sarabande, minuet, allemande, courante, gavotte, and so on. These forms proved highly adaptable for instrumental music that was meant for listening, not dancing— music played by a solo instrument like the violin or harpsichord,

Basso Continuo

During the Baroque period, instrumental ensembles almost always included a keyboard instrument, such as the harpsichord, to play chords. But the music for that instrument was not completely written out. Only a bass line—the lowest notes of the music—would be indicated, with a few written figures specifying what chords should go with those bass notes. The player would fill in the harmony freely, almost like a jazz musician, embellishing certain chords along the way as the mood struck. This process would continue throughout the piece (hence, the Italian term *continuo*). The keyboard was usually joined by a cello, which played the same bass line. These "continuo players" underline and flesh out the harmonic foundation of a composition; during oratorios, such as George Frideric Handel's *Messiah*, they also provide the accompaniment to "recitative" (passages of vocal music that introduce or separate solo arias and choral numbers). Skilled continuo players remain an essential ingredient in performances of Baroque music today.

or an ensemble. During the zenith of the Baroque era, the early 1700s, such masterworks as Handel's *Water Music* (so-called because it was first performed on a barge floating down the River Thames) demonstrated the versatility and expressive range of these dance forms.

By the late 1600s, the rising middle class in Europe developed a strong interest in music and helped bring it out of its exclusive salons and within reach of more ordinary folk. Concert societies, sometimes located in taverns, sprang up; eventually, the first concert halls—theaters built specifically for the public performance of what we call classical music—appeared. And musical

Talent and Coincidence

It so happens that the two most illustrious composers of the Baroque era, Bach and Handel, were born in the same year, 1685, just a few miles apart in Germany. As they matured into brilliant musicians, each was aware of the other, but the two never met. Curiously, both men developed cataracts in their last years and both were operated on, without success, by the same English doctor. When Bach died in 1750, essentially blind, he was hardly known to the music world at large; when Handel died in 1759, essentially blind, he was one of the best-known composers of his day. The music of each man is distinctive; a Bach composition can rarely be mistaken for one by Handel, and vice versa. But, together, they created the highest forms of expression in the Baroque age; each man, in his own way, defined that age.

ensembles, from amateur choral groups to orchestras of several dozen players, could be found almost everywhere. Chamber music—works for a small number of players, originally intended for private performance by amateurs or professionals in homes and other intimate spaces—became a popular social and artistic activity. Composers, seizing on the new possibilities for getting their music performed (and, thanks to improved printing processes, disseminated), made the first tentative steps away from private service at courts and churches and into the public cultural marketplace. The Baroque age also saw the rise of virtuoso performers, who displayed their sterling techniques and flair for embellishment (improvised ornamentation of melodic lines was a common occurrence) in concertos—works for solo instrument and orchestra. Singers, too, were expected to ornament their solos in oratorios—vast works on religious themes for soloists, chorus, and orchestra that became the rage (Handel was the preeminent oratorio composer of this period).

It was in the Baroque period that many of the fundamentals in Western music were established. In addition to the rules of harmony (including a clearly defined distinction between major and minor chords) and counterpoint, certain clear-cut musical structures became common and have served as models ever since. These include the sonata, a three-movement work for solo instrument, and the concerto, a three-movement work for solo instrument and orchestra.

Although people began to grow weary of the frilliness associated with the Baroque arts as the eighteenth century proceded, this dynamic style left a permanent mark on music history.

The Ideals of Classicism

The mid- and late-eighteenth century witnessed a new set of values that stressed clarity of line and directness of expression in art, architecture, and music. This was the rise of Classicism, a product of the Age of Enlightenment, with its emphasis on reason and balance. In this era, the polyphonic style gave way to a homophonic style—a predominant melodic line supported by harmony. The ear no longer had to contend with many ideas vying for attention simultaneously, but could focus easily on one at a time. And the practice of embellishing melodies was substantially curtailed for instrumentalists and singers alike to cut down on excess and unabashed bravura; moderation and restraint became the order of the day.

The new style is called "Classical" (which means that, technically, there's such a thing as Classical classical music). With this style came new musical structures emphasizing proportion

Embellishment

In some types of Baroque music, solo vocalists and instrumentalists were allowed—indeed, expected—to embellish or ornament the melodic line. As a rule, this occurred in compositions that involved the repetition of a particular section; the embellishment would come during the repeat. On the vocal side, such opportunities frequently come in oratorios with solo arias. A popular form of Baroque aria is called "da capo," which means "to the head"; the singer goes back to the beginning section of the aria and repeats it, changing the melody here and there with extra notes. There usually is a cadenza to cap such an aria—an a cappella passage when the soloist goes off on one final flight of musical fancy. Vocalists were not the only ones who got in on the fun; instrumentalists also had occasions to embellish melodic lines and to play cadenzas in concertos and other works. Things could get out of hand with this freedom. A violinist who got carried away spinning out an elaborate cadenza in a Handel composition heard directly from the composer himself when the cadenza finally ran out of steam—"Welcome home," Handel said in a voice the whole audience could hear.

The use of embellishment disappeared for a time; recordings of Handel arias made in the early 1900s, for example, rarely contain any ornamentation. But since the resurgence of interest in authentic performance practice that began in the 1960s, singers usually attempt some kind of melodic variation in da capo arias. It's still a wonderful opportunity to display technical versatility and expressive imagination, which is what audiences in the Baroque era craved.

and symmetry. The Baroque suite of several dance forms gave way to the standard, four-movement symphony. Although one of the old dances, the minuet, was retained in the symphony, the other movements usually followed new formulas. The most important of these is known as "sonata form" (not to be confused with plain old "sonata," a multiple-movement work for solo instrument). This form provided an outline that composers have used ever since—the "exposition" of two contrasting themes, the "development" of those themes, and the restating or "recapitulation" of them.

The unending inspiration of Joseph Haydn and Wolfgang Amadeus Mozart, the two giants of this age, yielded hundreds and hundreds of masterworks in the Classical style, filled with ingenious manipulation and development of engaging melodies. Composers in this period took full advantage of the ever-improving instruments available to them, including more colorful and dynamic keyboard instruments, and ever-expanding ensembles. The orchestra, which commonly had been around two dozen players in the Baroque days, doubled in the eighteenth century, and sometimes grew even larger.

The main keyboard instrument of the Classical era was the precursor of the piano, the fortepiano, an instrument with strings that were hammered rather than plucked, like the Baroque harpsichord, and that offered a wider palette of expressive shades. The string quartet—two violins, one viola, one cello—emerged as the most important grouping for chamber music, inspiring composers to write works that combined intimacy and intricacy, breadth and depth. Although many composers of the Classical era still relied on royal or ecclesiastical patronage to make a living, they welcomed new opportunities to earn money and reach a wider audience with a new outlet—the public concert. Concerts were often presented by a composer as a benefit—for himself (Mozart raised much-needed money this way). The late-eighteenth century also saw the beginning of "subscription concerts," a way of selling several performances for a single price; concert series to this day follow the practice.

Mannheim Mania

One of the first great orchestras to enter the scene was located in Mannheim, Germany, at the court of the elector of Mannheim, Carl Theodor, a sophisticated patron of the arts, especially music. His orchestra developed an enviable reputation for technical brilliance and for specific sound effects—the "Mannheim crescendo," a dramatic rise in volume; the "Mannheim rocket," a particular kind of melodic leap; even the "Mannheim sigh," the highly expressive articulation of little downward phrases that suggested a human sigh. Mozart was among the many composers who greatly admired this ensemble and the whole productive atmosphere of the court.

The Force of Romanticism

By 1800, the stage was set for the next era, the Romantic. It just needed a little push, which it got from Ludwig van Beethoven, the unique, stylistic link between Classicism and Romanticism. By the time he died in 1827, he had expanded every form that Haydn and Mozart had perfected as he sought ways of expressing his unusually bold emotions—anger, pride, passion, longing, love of nature, and idealism. His symphonies, sonatas, concertos, string quartets, and other works got longer and longer (the first movement alone of his Symphony no. 3 is as long as some four-movement symphonies from the Classical era). And the content of the music got more and more "in your face" (or at least in your ear); there is very little aural wallpaper in Beethoven's output. With such a piece as his Ninth Symphony, which broke all tradition by adding a chorus and four solo singers in the finale, Beethoven signaled decisively that classical music had no boundaries—and that Classicism was over.

The Romantic composers picked up on what Beethoven did and ran with it. Symphonies, concertos, sonatas, and chamber pieces grew even more directly expressive, with hearts on sleeves. Orchestras got bigger and bigger, reaching the one hundred–plus size still considered the norm today, and, as a result, the necessity for conductors became readily apparent.

The fortepiano of Mozart's day evolved during the nineteenth century into the concert grand piano seen on stages to this day; it became the dominant instrument of music, played in homes as well as on public stages. Felix Mendelssohn, Frederic Chopin, Robert Schumann, and Franz Liszt were among the composers who revealed the amazing world of sound and color possible from the piano. Wind instruments also were perfected; those that previously had no valves, like horns and trumpets, acquired them, making it easier to play more notes.

The nineteenth century saw the proliferation of concert halls, which brought music to the general public in numbers previously unimagined; the aristocracy may still have filled the box seats, but they were sharing the theaters with nearly every other class of society for the first time. Audiences had longer attention spans than today. From the dawn of public concerts in the late-eighteenth century and well into the nineteenth, concert programs were normally packed with music—a few overtures, maybe a couple of concertos, several arias from popular operas of the day, a choral work or two, and a symphony.

Another product of the Romantic age, with its embrace of individuality, was the solo recital—a performance by a single pianist or a soloist (such as a violinist or cellist) with piano

Ludwig van Beethoven

Although Beethoven technically preceded the Romantic era, he was very much embraced by the Romantics. He was so individualistic, his output so monumental, that he was seen as a kind of musical god. And to the Romantic mind, his deafness was a source of deep pathos. The story of the premiere of his Ninth Symphony in 1824 was well-loved. Beethoven had to be gently turned around onstage after the performance, which he could not hear, so that he could see the audience cheering wildly. That out of his internal darkness Beethoven could create such mighty symphonies and concertos was a source of reverential admiration for generations. But when faced with his last works, the unconventional piano sonatas and string quartets, the Romantics decided that Beethoven would never have produced such baffling, even disturbing harmonies and diffuse melodies, had he not been deaf. It took many years before the profound beauty and spiritual depth of those late pieces—the very qualities that linked them more directly with the ideals of Romanticism—were widely appreciated.

accompaniment. Recitals became a major draw with the public, leading to the emergence of classical music's first superstars, such as Liszt on the piano and Niccolo Paganini on the violin.

The classically trained singer, previously confined mostly to opera and/or sacred music, enjoyed an important new outlet during the Romantic era—the art song. German composers, especially, produced enormous quantities of art songs (*lieder* in German), using for texts the vivid verses of great (and sometimes minor) poets. This poetry reflected the major themes of the time, such as nature, ideal love, unrequited love, alienation, and nostalgia; the music intensified and illuminated those themes.

Follow the Leader

By the time of the Renaissance, a lot of music was being written for sizable groups of instruments, which led to the question of leadership. Up until around the beginning of the nineteenth century, an ensemble was typically led by one of the musicians playing in it, usually the first violinist or the keyboard player (a harpsichord or other keyboard instrument was almost always part of any group before 1800 or so). Gradually, the concept of a conductor took hold—someone whose chief function was to establish the tempo and keep everyone together. From the nineteenth century on, an additional function was common—interpretation, a personal approach to interpreting the notes on a page and getting an orchestra to realize it.

Being a conductor was not always easy in the early days. Jean-Baptiste Lully, a favorite composer at the court of Louis XIV, used a long cane with a rather sharp point at the end to beat out the tempo on the floor when he conducted his music. One day, while conducting a celebratory choral piece, he misjudged his aim and stuck his own foot with the stick. The resulting wound turned gangrenous and killed him a few weeks later. The chances for a similar fate to befall subsequent conductors grew slimmer after the baton—a thin, usually short stick waved in the air, away from body parts—became the norm in the 1800s and thereafter.

Franz Schubert, Schumann, and Johannes Brahms were among the most indelible lieder composers. Most of the other Romantic composers contributed to the art song repertoire; Peter Ilyich Tchaikovsky's output was particularly rich in emotion, as in the still-popular "None but the Lonely Heart," a perfect example of Romanticism in song.

Composers broke nearly all ties with palaces and cathedrals,

Concert Etiquette

Audiences have not always been on their best behavior at concerts, either in olden days or ours. Just as crowds at opera houses in the eighteenth century routinely chatted and dined their way through performances, people attending orchestral programs during the early days of public concerts, starting around the late 1700s, could be inattentive and distracting. They could also be demanding. If they liked something, they expected it to be encored. And they didn't feel particularly compelled to hear a long work in one continuous flow. A three-movement concerto, for example, might be broken up with a couple of arias sung by an opera star in between the movements. And when an audience did listen to a complete work, the crowd felt free to applaud after each movement. From the nineteenth century on, the public also felt free to boo or hiss when provoked by new sounds; this happened to works by several composers, such as Gustav Mahler, who eventually became very popular.

Over time, certain rules of etiquette for concertgoers have emerged. Audiences are expected to behave, to refrain from talking, eating, drinking, or wandering around. These days, unwrapping candy or letting cell phones and beepers go off is also sensibly discouraged. Over time, it became the norm to withhold applause in between the movements of a work, so that the music could be heard as a totality, not a succession of unrelated ideas. It's not an ironclad rule, however; certain movements with razzle-dazzle finishes (the first movement of Peter Ilyich Tchaikovsky's Piano Concerto no. 1, for example) almost guarantee an ovation, and few people would complain.

There can be a certain stuffiness about classical concerts as a result of such restrictions, and, for the newcomer, a feeling of intimidation. But the traditions are really just a matter of respect for the music and the musicians—and common politeness.

writing music on commission from instrumentalists, ensembles, and impresarios, or selling works directly to publishers. Those works throughout the mid- and late-1800s, like poetry and painting of the time, reflected widespread interest in nature, the supernatural, folk legends, exotic lands, and freedom—all reactions against the orderly, logical principles of the previous Age of Enlightenment. Romantics took delight in the unpredictability of the world, unexplained phenomena, and myth; they were fascinated as well with death and other dark thoughts that the Classicists would have avoided as much as possible.

Such compositions as the *Symphonie fantastique* ("Fantastic Symphony") by Hector Berlioz were the epitome of the Romantic style—big and often brash, filled with extra-musical associations that could never have made it into a symphonic work a generation earlier (the score tells the story of a lovesick man's hallucinations during an opium trip). The emergence of one-movement, often quite short, character-rich pieces demonstrated other Romantic traits and sentiments with such titles as "Ballade" and "Prelude" and "Impromptu," written by Chopin, Liszt, and others.

The nineteenth century saw the rise of nationalism throughout Europe as more and more people sought freedom from outside rule (the Austrian and French domination of Italy, for example) and espoused revolutionary, democratic ideals. Not surprisingly, composers reflected these new feelings and became increasingly identified by nationality; their styles reflected their own personal backgrounds to a degree previously uncommon. A century earlier, a composer from Scandinavia was likely to write music that sounded more or less the same as that by a composer from Italy. But in the Romantic age, no one mistook Russia's Tchaikovsky, Nicolai Rimsky-Korsakov, or Modest

Mussorgsky for Bohemia's Antonín Dvořák or England's Edward Elger. All of those composers drew on the same rich traditions of harmony and musical structure begun back in the Classical era, but each gave them a decidedly individualistic and ethnic stamp.

Throughout the nineteenth century, there was an enrichment of harmony to heighten expression, to extract greater feeling or deeper thought from music. Composers like César Franck picked up where Bach had left off and found fascinating ways to stretch harmonic progressions; Gabriel Fauré found increasingly elegant and subtle uses for this enhanced musical language. But no one provided a more dramatic jolt to the development of music in the century than Richard Wagner. In one way or another, his epic operas of the mid-1800s affected virtually all classical music of the time, and much of it afterward, generating fierce admirers and detractors. Wagner's extraordinarily rich chords and expectant melodies, capable of leading in many different directions and taking on many different emotional tints, gave fresh fuel to the Romantic movement.

Super Romanticism

As the twentieth century grew near, several composers were pushing what had been considered Wagner's extremes into even more complex harmonic fields and structural lengths. Symphonies by Anton Bruckner and Gustav Mahler, infused with Wagnerian resonances, aimed for universal truths or spiritual transcendence—and took their time seeking them. When Mahler said that a symphony should encompass the world, he wasn't kidding. His enormous scores called for such exotic sounds as cowbells and, within a single movement, could range

Nationalism

One of the most pronounced characteristics of nineteenth-century Romanticism was the rise in music that reflected specifically nationalistic characteristics. Music had previously been a predominantly abstract art; folk music was sometimes introduced, especially by Haydn, to add a character and charm. But music didn't become strongly linked to nationality until the Romantic age, when more and more composers asserted their individuality in fresh ways, especially through the use of musical ideas from their own native countries. Slavic and Scandinavian composers, in particular, frequently sought inspiration from the music of their own people. Folk songs and folk rhythms found their way into symphonies by Dvořák and Tchaikovsky and assorted works by Edvard Grieg, for example, providing them with a unique, vivid identity. In a way, Johann Strauss was a nationalist composer, too, earning his fame taking a dance in three-quarter time and making it distinctly, unmistakably Viennese. Manifestations of musical nationalism could be found in music from many countries throughout the nineteenth century and well into the twentieth.

in character from noble to vulgar. The orchestra size got even bigger for his nine symphonies; Mahler's Symphony no. 8 acquired the nickname "Symphony of a Thousand" because it called for an unusually large number of instrumentalists and vocalists. Also stretching the technical and expressive dimensions of the traditional orchestra were the brilliant "symphonic poems" by Richard Strauss, such as *Ein Heldenleben* ("A Hero's Life") and *Don Quixote*. Strauss and Mahler also had a more intimate side, carrying on the venerable tradition of German lieder with songs of exceptional poetic and musical sophistication.

While this super-Romantic expansion was evolving out of Wagner's musical legacy, there were also strong reactions *against* everything Wagner and his admirers created. The most notable opposition came in France. Claude Debussy, in particular, rejected Wagner's thick harmonies for exotic, Oriental ones, massive sonics for transparency of instrumental textures, and old-fashioned structures for unpredictable, even diffuse ones. Debussy and a few of his contemporaries were labeled "impressionists," for their music seemed to mirror the paintings of Monet and Renoir or the misty symbolism of such poets as Stéphane Mallarmé (who, along with Paul Verlaine and others, provided inspiration for many art songs of exquisite subtlety). Debussy's orchestral piece *Prelude to the Afternoon of a Faun* is a perfect example of Impressionism, a hazy, sensual painting in sound. Impressionistic music was less obvious, less clearly defined than what was coming out of Germany and Austria at the time; edges were blurred and softened. There was a play of light and shadows in these aural impressions, and a freedom of harmony and form that would lead to more experiments as the twentieth century unfolded.

The Experimental Century

In the early 1900s, different styles in classical music were all going strong—the final stages of Romanticism, as represented by the works of Mahler, Strauss, Jean Sibelius, Sergei Rachmaninoff, Edward Elgar, and others; and the twilight of Impressionism, as represented by Maurice Ravel, Erik Satie, Manuel de Falla, and others. Then, just before the start of the First World War, a spark of revolution hit classical music. It came in Paris at the premiere of a new ballet with music by

Igor Stravinsky called *The Rite of Spring*. The effect of this work's bold blast against musical convention would reverberate for decades.

The War to End All Wars, which did no such thing, did end a lot of traditions. Radical notions, wicked humor, dissonant sights and sounds followed quickly in the wake of that conflict as all of the arts underwent enormous changes in style, content, and emphasis. *The Rite of Spring* had paved the way for distrust of the old ways, the tired-and-true approaches to melody, harmony, and form. Now there was a widespread loosening of musical boundaries. Folk music had long ago burrowed its way into the classical scene, but it took on a much spicier quality now, especially in the works of a composer like Hungary's Béla Bártok. Ragtime (personified by Scott Joplin) and then jazz started infiltrating classical domains, producing startling examples of rhythmic vitality by Ravel, Stravinsky, and others, before reaching inventive heights with George Gershwin. He was one of several composers who would prove that Americans didn't have to settle for pale imitations of what European composers were doing. (In his own way, John Philip Sousa had already been doing that earlier with his unmistakably American marches. And Charles Ives had been busy at the turn of the century blazing fresh trails of harmony and form with the intrepidity of a true American pioneer, but his efforts wouldn't be widely appreciated until the 1950s.)

The aftermath of the war saw many sacred concepts about music crumble in Europe as composers caught up with the avant-garde, pre–World War I painters like Picasso and Braque. The Cubists had dared to abandon traditional perspective and look at every body part as equal when assembling a portrait, so it didn't make much difference where an ear or a mouth might

The Rite of Spring

Few premiere performances in music are as notorious as that of *The Rite of Spring (Le sacre du primtemps)*, with music by Igor Stravinsky and choreography by the legendary Nijinsky. Although the well-attended dress rehearsal took place without incident, the next night, May 29, 1913, at the Theatre des Champs-Elysees in Paris, was a much different story. The music never really had a chance as the audience erupted in riotous behavior almost from the first sounds from the orchestra pit and the first sights onstage. The ballet's earthy, violent tale, and Nijinsky's ideas on how to dance it probably had a lot to do with the public's reaction (the choreographer had to yell out the beats from backstage to the dancers, who could not hear the music because of the fracas). But what did come through over the din certainly fueled the battle. The score's savage rhythms, grating and weird sounds, odd twists and turns of melody proved disconcerting to many, including eminent French composer Camille Saint-Saens, who left early in a huff (his younger colleagues, Claude Debussy and Maurice Ravel, stayed and rallied the pro-*Rite* forces in the theater). There were reports of fisticuffs, spitting, slapping, and even some duel-threatening, but if Stravinsky's revolutionary score lost the first battle, it certainly won the war. Within a year, the music was performed sans ballet in Paris and generated an ecstatic reaction. No one has doubted its monumental originality and importance since.

be placed. It was the essence of the individual that mattered, conveyed in fresh ways, from fresh vantage points. In the 1920s, Arnold Schoenberg argued that music needed to be approached from a new perspective, too, one in which it didn't matter if notes sounded strange, out of place, out of normal context. Composers should no longer be slaves to old-fashioned harmony,

Schoenberg argued, so he declared the equality of all twelve tones in a traditional Western scale, which had for centuries been subservient to rules of harmony. His astonishing concept of how to base an entire composition on a preselected arrangement of those twelve tones threw the classical music world into a tizzy.

Schoenberg's complicated method, known as "twelve-tone music," attracted such imaginative disciples as Alban Berg and Anton Webern, and soon dominated thinking at major conservatories; among the most faithful adherents to the gospel of atonality have been such brilliant (and daunting) composers as Elliott Carter. But many twentieth-century composers refused to embrace the legacy of Schoenberg. Some, like Sergei Rachmaninoff and Ralph Vaughan Williams, remained basically rooted in warmhearted Romanticism. Others, like Dmitri Shostakovich, expanded on Mahler's sound world and created a deeply expressive and dramatic style. Others tried a return to the simplicity and directness of eighteenth-century music, filtered through twentieth-century ears; this elegant, sometime piquant style became known as "neo-classicism" (Stravinsky and Sergei Prokofiev championed the style for a while). Still others, notably Benjamin Britten, Aaron Copland, and Leonard Bernstein, incorporated all sorts of elements—folk music, jazz, Classicism, Romanticism—to produce their own strongly flavored, contemporary, accessible mix. Mavericks like Olivier Messiaen defied classification as they created distinctive sounds and structures that alternated between the simple and the exceedingly complex, all bathed in an aura of intense spirituality.

In short, what happened to music throughout that century can be neatly summed up by the 1960s expression "do your own thing." All sorts of styles and combinations of styles were tried, abandoned, and picked up again. John Cage, the most famous and provocative member of the avant-garde, argued that music should be defined broadly to include just about any sound, either made deliberately or by chance (the notes in one of his works were determined by a coin toss). Such experiments, along with multimedia pieces (music and film, for example) and electronic music generated by computers and synthesizers, provided potent weapons in the battle against conventionality. Much to the surprise of the public, which never did warm up to the Schoenberg legacy, the mid-twentieth century saw leading conservatories become strong advocates for "serial" music, turning out composers who embraced and intensified Schoenberg's methods to create works out of predetermined elements. Serialism was considered for a long time to be the pinnacle of intellectual and musical thought.

Not surprisingly, there came a strong, fascinating reaction against serialism—indeed, against just about everything that had been going on in the century. This countermovement began to make big waves in the 1970s, when the word *minimalism* entered the musical vocabulary. This style relied on a minimum of ingredients. A tiny snippet of melody, a few simple chords, a chugging rhythm—all repeated over long stretches of time— were all such leading minimalists as Philip Glass, Steve Reich, and John Adams needed. Great debates over the style raged, but many audiences welcomed this slap in the face at a variety of musical conventions.

Classical Music at the Millennium

With the start of the twenty-first century, a wide range of musical styles from previous decades can still be heard. Several composers, such as Pierre Boulez, Luciano Berio, and Hans Werner Henze, remain largely immersed in highly complex, atonal, serial styles that have roots stretching back to Schoenberg's revolution. John Corigliano, Ellen Taaffe Zwilich, Richard Danielpour, and several more turn out music with strong melodic lines, familiar harmonies, and clear structures that suggest a new brand of Romanticism. Meanwhile, Glass, Reich, and Adams entered the new century writing works that are in many ways quite different from what they first produced, but the richer layers of melody, rhythm, and texture have not disguised their minimalist roots. And the spiritual element in music, which had been so imaginatively explored by Messiaen, remains an important concern for men like John Tavener and Avro Pärt.

Further evolution will go on as composers make the most of their freedom to explore, refine, shake up, toss out, and renew. Yet, chances are, we will still find a connective thread to the past somewhere in any new style that may come along. For all of the varied means of expression already out there, it's amazing how many of the familiar structures of music that served Bach and Mozart and Beethoven and Brahms and Tchaikovsky remain in use. The sounds may have changed a lot over the centuries, but not the basic beauty and power—and infinite possibilities—of classical music.

THREE

Varieties of Classical Music

Classical music can be broken down into several broad areas, reflecting either historical time period or stylistic characteristics—or both. These categories form part of the everyday jargon of classical music. They do not involve ironclad distinctions and restrictions, but rather provide a convenient way of generalizing and grouping.

The varieties described here are among the most common that a Curious Listener will encounter, but this list is neither objective nor comprehensive. For example, opera is certainly a type of classical music, written by classical composers and performed by classically trained singers. But it is ordinarily treated as an entirely separate universe since it involves theater as well as music, so it is not listed here. Other forms of vocal music, however, are included.

Becoming familiar with these general varieties should provide a firm stepping-off point for a deeper look into the who, what, how, and why of classical music.

Art Songs: It would be misleading to think of art songs as the opposite of popular songs, since many art songs are popular and many pop songs are very artistic. But there is something decidedly different about an art song, even if it has a very direct melody and simple harmony. The style of composition, the nature of the words, and the careful writing out of the accompaniment part—not to mention the need for a classically trained singer—place an art song in a decidedly separate category. Since the late eighteenth century, many composers have contributed to this genre, but the heyday for art songs came in the nineteenth, during the Romantic era, when poetry was a particularly powerful force in literature. Many composers were drawn to the writings of leading (and sometimes lesser) poets of the day, and set their verses to music for voice and accompaniment (almost always piano). Among the greatest composers of art songs were Franz Schubert, Robert Schumann, Gabriel Fauré, Claude Debussy, and Richard Strauss.

Atonal Music: Atonal music is a provocative style of music in which traditional Western concepts of harmony and tonality, the sense of harmonic order and logic, are abandoned. The result is what the average ear will hear, at least initially, as dissonance. Instead of the clear-cut world of C major (do, re, mi, fa, sol, la, ti, do), there is no sense of a specific key. Various systems of atonal music have been tried out. Some composers have made limited use of atonality within compositions that are otherwise tonal; others make an effort to banish all trace of conventional harmonic progression. The most devoted atonalists usually follow a set of rules, first espoused by Arnold Schoenberg in the 1920s, that guarantees freedom from the old methods of building chords or shaping melodic lines. Atonal music typically involves awkward leaps between notes, dense chords, and complex rhythmic changes.

Contrary to popular opinion, atonality is not inherently ugly or harsh. Many atonal composers wrote as expressively as the most determined of Romantics, and laid out their musical structures as painstakingly and logically as the most ardent Classicists. A committed performance of an atonal composition can be deeply beautiful and meaningful, just as abstract paintings can be.

Baroque Music: "Baroque" is not the most precise of terms, but it has come to signify music from roughly the seventeenth century to the middle of the eighteenth, from Claudio Monteverdi and Jean-Philippe Rameau to Johann Sebastian Bach, George Frideric Handel, Arcangelo Corelli, Domenico Scarlatti, Antonio Vivaldi, and Georg Philipp Telemann. Somewhat like Baroque architecture, with its curving lines and elaborate features, Baroque music has an element of complexity and intricacy.

The most obvious characteristics of Baroque music are rhythmic motion, counterpoint, and singleness of focus. As a rule, a Baroque piece is going to be in constant motion; even a slow movement in a concerto, for example, will have a steady flow. And you can usually count on imitative counterpoint—two or more independent melodic lines chasing after each other, imitating the first melodic line that is sounded. These multiple lines overlap, often in very complicated ways, yet fit together cohesively. Virtually all Baroque music employs some form of counterpoint; even a keyboard piece will have it, with the right hand and left hand doing their own involved things, instead of the right hand getting all the melody and the left merely playing chords. As for the singleness of focus, Baroque composers conceived of music in highly unified ways. Each piece, or each movement of a multiple-movement work, almost always is held together by one primary melodic idea (or even just a single rhythmic pattern) that is inventively developed, and by one tempo. These restrictions did not limit a good composer's imagination, but, rather, unleashed it.

A piece of Baroque music is like a journey that starts at home, travels down many a winding road and unexpected curve, but invariably finds its way safely back. No matter how complicated the music may get along the way, the sense of resolution at the end will be very clear and very satisfying.

Chamber Music: Chamber music gets a bad rap from some folks, who think it isn't exciting or loud enough, or doesn't have enough going on in it. A little experience with it will belie that notion. Chamber music is one of the most intimate and rewarding genres of classical music to perform and to hear.

Ordinarily, compositions that require from two (duo) to eight (octet) or nine (nonet) players—with each one having a separate part to play—are categorized as chamber music.

The "chamber" in chamber music goes back to the origin of the genre, when small groups of musicians played in small spaces—private rooms, or chambers. There was a social function to these gatherings, too; musicians—amateurs or professionals—were brought together in a closely knit experience of sonic bonding. Eventually, chamber music attracted avid listeners as well as performers; by the start of the nineteenth century, chamber music was moving into public concert halls. In our day, chamber music groups often perform in very large halls, where feelings of intimacy between musicians and audiences are limited.

Although written on a small scale, compared to orchestral repertoire, chamber music is hardly limited in terms of melodic richness, rhythmic motion, dramatic impact, or instrumental coloring. As with so many things, size definitely does not matter. Some listeners, reared on the thicker sound of orchestras, may have trouble adjusting, but it's worth the effort.

The preeminent type of chamber music is the string quartet, equal in artistic weight to a symphony for full orchestra. Like the symphony, a quartet (two violins, viola, and cello) usually has four movements, arranged as they are in a symphony. And like chamber music in general, a quartet provides a vehicle of intense and intimate interaction among a small ensemble of players. Joseph Haydn and Wolfgang Amadeus Mozart elevated the quartet to a particularly high level of inspiration, finding innumerable ways of using only four instruments to convey eloquent musical thoughts. Ludwig van Beethoven took the quartet even further, calling for exceptional virtuosity in some cases and great sensitivity in others. His final quartets, which baffled many musicians and listeners for years, reveal an eloquence and profundity, as well as a stretching of form and harmony, that still sounds amazingly fresh and inventive. Quartets by Franz Schubert, Johannes Brahms, and Antonín Dvořák rank among the hallmarks of the Romantic era. In the twentieth century, Dmitri Shostakovich used the string quartet to express some of his deepest, darkest thoughts.

Although the first violin part often carries the bulk of the melodic lines in a quartet, and the others provide harmony, most composers take full advantage of all four instruments; solos for viola and cello are especially common, and even the second violin will often step into the limelight. By the use of pizzicato (a plucking of the strings, instead of bowing), mutes (clamps placed on the strings to soften the sound), and other devices, a composer can provide a great array of aural interest out of four intrinsically similar instruments.

Other compositions for small groups of string instruments include the string trio (violin, viola, and cello, or two violins and cello), string quintet (two violins, two violas, and cello, or two violins, viola, and two cellos) and string sextet (pairs of violins, violas, and cellos). The keyboard is often added to strings to form other types of ensembles: the piano trio (violin, cello, piano), the piano quartet (violin, viola, cello, piano), and the piano quintet (string quartet and piano). Wind instruments also are featured in chamber works, sometimes with strings and/or piano, sometimes by themselves.

Making things slightly confusing is that types of chamber music also identify the kind of ensemble that plays them; the terms are interchangeable. So a string quartet performs string quartets, a piano trio performs piano trios, etc.

Classical Music: *Classical*—with a capital *C*—is not the same as the generic term *classical music*. This is music from a specific time period. Music of the Classical period, stretching from the mid-1700s to the early 1800s and represented by such giants as Joseph Haydn and Wolfgang Amadeus Mozart, shed many of the complexities of the Baroque. Instead of counterpoint—multiple, independent lines—there was a move toward a single melodic line taking prominence and supported by clear-cut harmony. And instead of developing a whole piece out of one melodic idea, as Baroque composers routinely did, contrast was introduced; there would be a principal theme and a secondary theme, each with its own characteristics.

Where the Baroque era produced music that could be as elaborate and confusing as Baroque architecture, the Classical era yielded music as perfectly proportioned as Classical architecture. A Georgian-style house, with its equally divided number of windows or doors and clean lines, found a sonic equivalent in compositions created with neatly symmetrical numbers of measures and a balance of thematic ideas. Elegance of expression was emphasized over the sometimes florid style of the Baroque. Restrained emotion, directness, clarity, and beauty of thought—these were the hallmarks of the Classical style.

Haydn was the quintessential classicist, producing an extraordinary number of perfectly reasoned works in all forms, from string quartet and keyboard sonata to concerto and symphony (he wrote more than one hundred). Mozart also represents the Classical ideal; the symmetrical shape of his melodic lines never fails to impress. His output was astonishingly consistent in quality; his piano concertos and symphonies attest most indelibly to that. When Ludwig van Beethoven arrived on the scene at the end of the eighteenth century, he was a Classicist, but he began to reveal hints of the Romantic style to come as he entered the nineteenth century.

Early Music: This handy, catchall term is often used to describe just about anything composed before the seventeenth century. This includes the limited amount of music that has come down to us from the Middle Ages—such things as Gregorian chant and troubadour songs—and on into the great musical flourishing of the Renaissance period. Among the major figures of early music are Hildegard of Bingen from the twelfth century, known for her almost transcendental chants; Guillaume de Machaut from the fourteenth century, important for his introduction of polyphony and rhythmic syncopation; and Josquin Desprez, who spanned the fifteenth and sixteenth centuries and achieved a mastery of polyphonic writing and a spirituality of expression.

Impressionism: Impressionism is a style that emerged in France toward the end of the nineteenth century. Instead of expanding on traditional Western harmony, as Richard Wagner and others did in the Romantic movement, the Impressionists, led by Claude Debussy (who never really liked that term), based much of their harmony on music from the Orient. The result was a rather exotic sound. Chords did not resolve the way Western ears expected them to; melodies unfolded in likewise unpredictable directions.

These Oriental touches created a softer-edged, hazy world of fresh, aural colors that suggested the equivalent of landscapes by Monet. Where the Romantics wrote so much that was in a totally overt, grab-you-by-the-ear manner, the Impressionists took a generally subtler approach, creating musical impressions instead of emphatic statements.

Minimalism: This provocative style of music, which began attracting attention in the 1960s and flourished wildly in the next few decades, owes something to Eastern music and to Western rock music. In a complete rejection of atonality and the complex method of composing known as serialism, for many years considered to be gospel in most music conservatories, minimalist composers went back to the basics. Simple, tonal chords replace dense, dissonant ones; melodic lines are likewise direct; a basic, rhythmic pattern, repeated over and over (sometimes with understated variations), propels the piece. A hypnotic effect can be achieved by the constant reiteration of melody, harmony, and rhythm.

Initially, minimalist works tended to avoid lyricism and other aspects of Romanticism, but as the style underwent constant refinement, new levels of expressive intensity were added. Where the first minimalist works got maximum mileage out of one, two, or three chords, more recent examples contain considerable harmonic action. And where melodies were very compact at first, they became increasingly expansive. But the sense of reiterative rhythmic motion has, for the most part, remained a primary element in minimalism.

Starting around 1960, two American avant-garde composers, La Monte Young and Terry Riley, experimented with what would become known as minimalism. Riley's 1965 composition "In C" epitomized the principles of the new style—the piece "for variable ensemble" calls for an indefinite repetition of series of musical motives, all centering on the key of C major. The most successful practitioners of the minimalist style are Steve Reich, Philip Glass, and John Adams. Although the three share certain traits in common, there is no mistaking one for another; their individuality speaks to the wide possibilities of expression under the minimalist banner.

Program Music: This term refers to compositions that tell a story of some kind through music, without words; there is a "program" behind the notes. This extra-musical idea may have to do with a work of literature or visual art, or perhaps just a philosophical idea; it might be inspired by nature, a dream, or an event in history. The concept of program music goes back centuries. There are, for example, keyboard pieces from the 1500s that attempt to describe famous battles. In the early 1700s, Antonio Vivaldi wrote his famous set of violin concertos called *The Four Seasons*; he attached a poem to each movement describing specific activity and feelings related to the time of year. The music helps to convey those images, often very realistically.

By the nineteenth century, the concept of program music advanced considerably. Beethoven's Symphony no. 6, known as the *Pastoral*, conveys a sense of the emotions aroused by a trip to the countryside; sounds of nature—bird calls, a flowing brook, a thunderstorm—are vividly represented in the music. Hector Berlioz took things a big step forward with his *Symphonie fantastique*. This "Fantastic Symphony" conveys the narrative of a forlorn lover who gets wasted on opium as he pines for the woman who got away; eventually, he has some pretty wild hallucinations that the prismatic music makes almost tangible. Among other notable program music composers were Franz Liszt and Richard Strauss, who perfected a particular form of the genre called a tone poem or symphonic poem, a work often in one movement for large orchestra that focuses on a single nonmusical subject. Antonín Dvořák, Bedrich Smetana, and Peter Ilyich Tchaikovsky, to name a few other obvious examples, also created memorable tone poems. Tchaikovsky's popular *1812* Overture is one of the best known pieces of program music, with its noisy depiction of battles between French and Russian armies; Modest Mussorgsky's *Night on Bald Mountain*, a vivid evocation of a witches' sabbath, and *Pictures at an Exhibition*, a musical tour of an actual art exhibit the composer attended, are equally celebrated cases of programmatic music.

Renaissance Music: Renaissance music encompasses a remarkable variety and quality of works that were, in their way, as brilliant and expressive as the art, architecture, and literature of the period. The polyphonic style of multiple melodic lines that had begun to flower in the late Middle Ages bloomed fully during this vital era, leading to some of the most enriching music ever written. Instrumental music also flourished, helping to provide certain foundations, especially of structure, for the next era, the Baroque, to build upon. Leading lights of the Renaissance included Giovanni Pierluigi da Palestrina, whose brilliant, deeply moving church music in sixteenth-century Italy inspired generations of composers; Andrea and Giovanni Gabrielli, the former renowned for his stereophonic placement of instrumental and vocal ensembles in different corners of St. Mark's Cathedral in Venice, the latter for his intensely expressive style; and William Byrd and Thomas Tallis, whose sophisticated, yet directly communicative church music provided high points of the English Renaissance.

Romantic Music: Where the movement known as Classicism yielded music of restraint and clear-cut order, Romanticism, which emerged in the early nineteenth century, generated music that reveled in emotional outpourings and unpredictability (a new, free-form piece introduced in this era was the "Impromptu"). The heart, which had been kept politely under control a generation earlier, now was worn on the sleeve. Instrumental music that had been abstract now became more specific in its content—downright literal in the case of "program music," works intended to convey extra-musical ideas,

narratives, pictures, etc. The Classical era had seen the introduction of musical contrast—different themes introduced in a
single movement; the Romantic era intensified those contrasts.
There were extremes of volume and tempo to enhance more
overtly expressive melodies and more daring harmonies (Richard Wagner, in his operas, opened the path toward those new
harmonies, a path many composers gleefully followed). There
also were extremes of length; some works, especially symphonies, were longer than any instrumental works written before.
(On the other side of the coin, you can find examples, like
certain piano pieces by Frederic Chopin or art songs by Robert
Schumann, that are unusually short, conveying a remarkable
amount of feeling in the equivalent of a single breath.)

Romantic music, represented by the likes of Hector Berlioz,
Johannes Brahms, Peter Ilyich Tchaikovsky, and Antonín
Dvořák, is unmistakable in its lyricism and power of expression,
with melodies that stick in the ear and try to stir up strong
feelings. The appeal of this style lasted well into the twentieth
century. Several of the composers who straddled the nineteenth
and twentieth centuries are often categorized under the heading
of post- or late-Romanticism—Gustav Mahler, Richard Strauss,
and Jean Sibelius, for example. The major elements of Romanticism remain in their works, but are articulated in an even
more complex and colorful language of melody and harmony.
Several composers in our day, rejecting the atonal style that was
dominant for a good portion of the twentieth century, have
created a new kind of Romanticism, a style that relies heavily
on directly expressive melodies and more or less traditional harmony, while incorporating contemporary musical spices.

Sacred Music: In the broadest sense, this term can be used to describe hymns and other pieces sung by congregations and church choirs during services. In the classical music realm, there are a lot of compositions with religious texts (primarily of Christian faiths) that have crossed over from church service into the concert hall because of their quality and wide appeal. Such music is generally referred to as "sacred," because of the subject matter, but requires no religious affiliation to appreciate. Verdi, for example, was little more than an agnostic personally, but produced one of the supreme examples of sacred music in his Requiem, which he never intended to be performed during an actual service. Bach's cantatas, first sung during services in the Lutheran church where he was employed, are now almost always presented out of that context. Masses by Haydn, Mozart, and Franz Schubert are rarely heard during an actual celebration of the Catholic Mass, as they first were, but in secular concerts. Once removed from liturgical settings, sacred music can be savored as pure music, enjoyed for beauty of melody, clarity of structure, and depth of expressive feeling.

Although Latin was the most frequently used language in sacred music from the Middle Ages through the nineteenth century, the genre has produced works in a variety of languages. Most of Bach's sacred works are in German, for example.

Among common forms of sacred music are Mass (consisting of traditionally sung portions of the Latin text for a Catholic service); Requiem (the text from the Latin Mass for the Dead); *Te Deum* (an extended hymn of praise and thanks); *Gloria* (a portion of the traditional Mass often set by itself as a composition); Passion (the story of the final days of Jesus, taken from one of the gospels); and Vespers (various prayers for an evening service).

Serialism: *Serialism* is a term used to define a specific type of atonal music developed primarily in the 1940s. It is often used interchangeably with the term *twelve-tone music*, the method developed by Arnold Schoenberg (see below). Ordinarily, this method of composition starts, like twelve-tone music, with a predetermined sequence (or series—hence, "serial") made up of the twelve tones in the Western chromatic scale (all the notes between an octave). All of the melodic lines and chords are then derived from the row in very specific, systematic, almost mathematical ways, without regard to tonal rules of harmony. In most serial music, however, that's only the beginning of the predetermined elements in the composition. It is also common to use the initial series to derive in advance the rhythms, dynamics (loud and soft), note values (how short or long a note is sounded), and other aspects that will characterize the work. Such an approach is called "total serialism," and goes far beyond what Schoenberg first envisioned. Because of its atonality and density of content, serial music has never enjoyed wide popularity, but several composers, notably Pierre Boulez and Milton Babbitt, have created fascinating, ear- and mind-opening works in the serial style.

Symphonic Music: Broadly speaking, this term refers to music performed by a full orchestra (sometimes called a "symphony orchestra"). One obvious example of such music is a symphony, a multiple-movement work. But single-movement pieces, such as tone poems and overtures, also qualify as symphonic music, again because of the performing forces involved.

Tonal Music: Tonal music defines the largest amount of Western classical music, from ancient times to our own. Tonality involves the use of what are called keys—C major, D minor, etc.—to create a sense of a harmonic home for the ear. A tonal piece, more often than not, will center on a home key, moving away at times into other keys (other chords), but eventually returning.

(As occurs so often in music, there can be some confusion about the term *key*. There are keys on a piano, for example, the actual pieces of wood that, when pressed down, cause a hammer to strike strings inside the instrument, producing a tone or a note. The other definition of "key" is a little more complicated. A specific group of notes that form a scale will, in turn, help to define a key. Here's an example: All the white notes on a piano from middle C to the next highest or lowest C would constitute a C-major scale, and the notes of that scale are the building blocks that create the key of C major.)

The concept of tonality evolved over several centuries. By the time of the Renaissance, this concept was becoming well entrenched. In addition to the standardization of keys, there was a general acceptance of relationships between keys. It is out of those relationships that the concept of tonality becomes richer. In tonal music, generally speaking, there is a progression of harmonies that relate to each other and make aural sense with each other. This harmonic progression is what helps to give the music interest, movement, and even mood and character. Tonal music—virtually all pop music is tonal, by the way—is what Western listeners have long regarded as normal. It is practically imbedded in our genes. If someone were to sing for you a C-major scale—do, re, mi, fa, sol, la, ti, do—but stop before the last note (the second, higher "do"), you would automatically hear that note in your head; you would be pulled toward it. That explains a little something about the nature of tonality and the relationships between notes and keys. Going from that "ti" to the final "do" is a form a resolution, of proclaiming a tonal center, in this case anchored by "do." This example merely scratches the surface of what is involved in tonality, but should be helpful in conveying the gist.

Twelve-Tone Music: Twelve-tone music is the name commonly used to describe a specific compositional system developed in the 1920s by Arnold Schoenberg. It also came to be called "serial music," though that term can encompass other theories of how to make music. Schoenberg's method revolutionized musical thinking and influenced composers for several decades.

The twelve tones of Western music can perhaps be best illustrated on a piano. Find middle C. Play that note and the next eleven going up the keyboard. These twelve notes—all the white and black keys starting from that middle C—constitute what is called a chromatic scale, the chief building block used for centuries in the creation of Western music. Schoenberg's twelve-tone method called for composers to select a sequence of those notes (without repeating any); this is called a tone row. Once the row has been determined, the entire melodic and harmonic elements of the piece will flow from that row according to complex, highly sophisticated rules. The row can be used backward or upside down (reversing the distance between each note), or upside down and backward.

Although the composer is not entirely free when writing twelve-tone music, the possibilities for individual expression remain limitless, beginning with the choice of a tone row and extending through all of the other areas of composition—form, dynamics, instrumentation, etc. The best twelve-tone composers produce works that sound genuinely expressive, even spontaneous, rather than academic and calculated.

FOUR

Classical Music Deconstructed

C lassical music involves two broad arenas—composition and performance. Both come with considerable challenges, not to mention rewards. The composer has to
decide any number of questions about a piece of music—form,
length, mood, and instrumentation; the performer has to consider how to interpret the composer's blueprint (or black-and-
white print), how closely to observe tempo indications, and how
to shape a phrase.

In the end, the principal concern for both the creator and
the re-creator is to make an artistic statement that has validity
and quality. The following pages offer a glimpse into the mechanics of making such a statement. In breaking down—de-
constructing—a few of the formidable component parts that go
into composition and performance, the Curious Listener may
find that classical music is a surprisingly approachable, under-
standable art form after all.

Musical Languages

Composers operate within certain parameters, the two most obvious being language and structure. What's a musical language? Basically, it's a characteristic that helps to define the style of a composition. Tonality is a language; so is atonality. In addition to those general languages, there are more detailed ones in Western music—three fundamental means of expression:

Monophony: Monophony involves a single melodic line, whether sung or played on an instrument, without any accompaniment. No harmony, no chords. Think Gregorian chant.

Homophony: Homophony also places the attention on a single melodic line, but has harmony underneath. Every pop song is homophonic.

Polyphony: Polyphony calls for the melodic activity to be spread among many independent, often equally important lines. Think Johann Sebastian Bach. But also think of those Mozart and Beethoven symphonies; they often use polyphonic techniques, too.

In certain periods of history, composers "spoke" only one musical language, either because another had not evolved or one was simply predominant and expected. But for centuries now, composers have been free to write in more than one style, to use whatever they wanted, when and how they wanted it.

Polyphony is the most difficult of these languages or styles to master, but just about every composer since the late seventeenth century has been expected to study it, and most of them have employed it. There is a defining element in the polyphonic style:

Counterpoint: Counterpoint was the principal musical technique from the Renaissance until roughly the mid-eighteenth century. If you think of the phrase "point-counterpoint," you can get a quick idea of how contrapuntal music works. Two or more musical lines go their separate ways, yet intersect and interact at certain spots. The music is always in motion. Counterpoint usually incorporates some form of imitation—the first melodic line will be imitated, more or less, by the next line that enters. There is a very simple form of imitative counterpoint, one you probably participated in as a kid. Think "Three Blind Mice."

Musical Structures

Just as a painter must decide on the size of a canvas and the scope of the intended image, and a sculptor must come to terms with the mass of material to be shaped into an object of art, a composer has to determine the formal characteristics of the piece at hand. This doesn't have to result in a terribly restrictive situation. Composers of Gregorian chant centuries ago were quite free in terms of how long their melodies might be; composers since the twentieth century have toyed with all sorts of seemingly formless forms, trying to change expectations about beginning, middle, and end. But somewhere, somehow, the music takes a shape; there is a kind of frame around it, helping to define it, at least partly.

The great majority of compositions that are listened to regularly have a very clear structure. And the more a listener knows about the common structures of music, the more the sounds will mean. Learning to dissect even a couple of these structures can make it a lot easier to absorb unfamiliar ones.

Let's go back to counterpoint—and your childhood:

Round: In the simplest counterpoint, one voice (this term is used generically to mean a melodic line, either sung or played by an instrument or by one hand at a keyboard) will start off with a tune; another voice will imitate it, starting on the same pitch, shortly afterward, blending into the picture. Then another voice does the same, and another, and another, with no predetermined ending. This is called a "round," best illustrated every time a group of kids sings "Row, Row, Row Your Boat," "Three Blind Mice" or "Frere Jacques."

Canon: A more sophisticated type of imitative counterpoint is the "canon." Here, the second voice may enter at the same pitch or another pitch, thus adding a new harmonic twist to the proceedings. And in a canon there is a clear ending, written in such a way to help any imitating lines catch up and contribute to a satisfying rounding-off of the music. You can find fascinating examples of canons in Bach's *Goldberg* Variations; every third variation is in the form of a canon. Bach shows off his skill even more by making the second voice of each canon enter on a progressively higher pitch. Canon writing went out of fashion after the Baroque era, but you will come across canons every now and then in works by composers as diverse as Joseph Haydn, César Franck, and Arnold Schoenberg.

Fugue: The fugue is the most complex form of imitative counterpoint, and was also a specialty of the Baroque period and of

Bach. A wag once described a fugue as a musical form in which one voice enters at a time—and one member of the audience leaves at a time. Sure enough, a concert devoted exclusively to fugues will not draw hordes of eager listeners, but that's no fault of the fugues. In the Baroque era, the fugue emerged as one of the highest forms of musical thought, the equivalent of a philosophical dissertation on logic. There is an academic aspect to the fugue, to be sure, in the sense that it involves a kind of puzzle that must be carefully worked out. Still, the great composers produced fugues that are not dry at all, but vibrant works that engage the mind and ear alike. The fugue is the ultimate in creating a musical form through the process of imitation.

The opening of a fugue, called a "subject," will be sounded by one voice. The subject may be of any length and might not even be particularly melodic, but perhaps infused with a distinctive rhythmic pattern, or perhaps creating an interesting arch out of a few, long-held notes. The subject will then receive an "answer"—another statement of the subject starting on a different pitch (not an arbitrary choice, but a pitch that provides a particular harmonic relationship to the key of the subject—don't worry, this sort of technical stuff is not necessary to the enjoyment of a fugue). Meanwhile, that first voice, having finished with the subject, is off into something else, called the "counter-subject," which provides counterpoint, a counter-argument to that second voice's entry. These two tightly interwoven voices will work their way back to the original harmonic center (the key) of the fugue so that—you guessed it—a third voice can enter the fray with yet another statement of the subject.

There may be still one more voice waiting its turn, too. After all the voices have jumped in with the subject, the composer goes to town developing all the material—subject and counter-subject—and probably adding in some fresh ideas as well. The harmony will keep changing as the development continues; the subject might get turned upside down or even played backward as the composer demonstrates his tricks of the trade. The ear may not pick up on all of this, but a good fugue lets you sense the playfulness, the creativity involved. Eventually, the music will move back to that starting key for one last hurrah with the subject and a solid wrapping up of the contrapuntal argument.

Bach never ran out of inspiration for fugal writing. Each of his two books of keyboard pieces called *The Well-Tempered Clavier* contains twenty-four pairs of preludes (free-form pieces) and fugues, one in each key (C major, C minor, D major, D minor, etc.).

You'll also encounter fugues in innumerable other works from virtually every composer of the Baroque period. Eventually, as musical styles changed in subsequent eras, fugues became less common as stand-alone pieces. They still showed up, though, especially in choral works (usually at the end of a large movement in a mass or requiem) of the eighteenth and nineteenth centuries, and also in the middle of a movement from a sonata or concerto or symphony as a means for a composer to develop themes. In the twentieth century, the great Russian composer Dmitri Shostakovich paid tribute to Bach and the art of the fugue with his own set of twenty-four preludes and fugues.

Fugues can become descriptive devices, too. The orchestral fugue at the start of Puccini's opera *Madame Butterfly*, for example, suggests the different forces at work preparing for the title character's wedding; a fugue in the finale of Tchaikovsky's

Manfred Symphony (based on Lord Byron's epic poem) repre-sents the world of academics that the hero of the piece rejects.

The more familiar the Curious Listener becomes with the process, logic, and craftsmanship of a fugue, the more beautiful and meaningful this landmark structure of classical music will become.

Bach's own sons were among the composers who began to seek a simpler musical language, moving away from counter-point and intricate polyphony; they also helped to create new forms to use with the new, more direct musical language that was evolving. One form, in particular, became dominant:

Sonata Form: Of all the musical structures over the centuries, this may be the most important. It has been in use since the mid-1700s, turning up as the first movement of one symphony after another, one string quartet after another; it can also be found in an overture, a concerto, a sonata—just about anything. There is one little problem about sonata form, though—the name. Go back one sentence and you'll see the word *sonata*. In that con-text, it refers to a multiple-movement work for solo instrument, or solo instrument and accompaniment (a sonata for violin and piano, for example). Since the first movement of a sonata can be in sonata form, things can get a little confusing. But don't give up. Try this analogy: If a sonata were a four-story building, sonata form would be the first floor. Once you've got the dis-tinction between sonata and sonata form down, the rest is a breeze.

In the Baroque era, composers really needed only one theme at a time; once they had a good tune and developed it as far as they could, they called it a day—or a movement. The first movement of Bach's *Brandenburg* Concerto no. 3, for example, boils down to one theme that is brilliantly tossed back and forth in contrapuntal fashion, turned every which way; there is essentially one tempo, one mood, and one color to the movement. That's the case with most Baroque music. One of the big changes in the next musical era, when Classicism reigned, was the introduction of contrasting themes within a single movement. And this is where sonata form comes in.

There are three parts to sonata form: exposition, development, and recapitulation. The composer begins by "exposing" a principal theme and then a secondary theme (exposition). The principal theme is likely to be vigorous, the secondary one more lyrical, providing the ear with a clear contrast. For a long time, it was customary to repeat the exposition, a nice benefit for those in the audience who arrived late or weren't paying attention the first time around. Then the composer "develops" the material from the exposition; perhaps just the first theme, or just the second, or both (development). In this section of the movement, the composer's imagination (or lack of it) will be most apparent. In an inspired development section, the themes from the exposition are cast in a new light, with all sorts of changes in character, coloring and harmony; it's a little like a jazz musician's improvisation on a tune, only all written down, of course. When the development is over, the material of the exposition—the principal and secondary themes—will return, more or less as at the start (recapitulation). A recapitulation is not necessarily the very end of the sonata form; a coda—a final wrapping up, which may or may not use material from the rest of the movement—is likely to be the last word, or note.

As has been the case all through music history, the great composers did not merely follow the rules, but made the rules follow them. So you can find incredible variety among applications of sonata form. Haydn, for example, occasionally took delight in making the principal and secondary themes sound virtually the same. Mozart would sometimes get to the development section and decide he didn't really feel like developing either of his themes, so he might seize on something else—a seemingly incidental phrase, a little filler from the exposition—or maybe even toss in a brand-new theme, and then give us a perfectly normal recapitulation. In the nineteenth century, several composers tried out a compression effect: The development and the recapitulation would, in effect, be combined.

The standard practice for composers from the late seventeenth century on through the nineteenth was to start a multiple-movement work with sonata form. But the form is so effective for organizing musical ideas that composers often have used it for more than one movement of the same piece. In Beethoven's Fifth Symphony, you'll find sonata form in the first, second, and fourth movements. And although musical styles changed drastically after Mozart's time, the sonata form remained a favorite device for composers right on through the twentieth century and will surely find many advocates in the twenty-first.

Speaking of "movements," just what does this term mean? It's generic for a self-contained section of a work with several such sections, analogous to the chapters in a book. And, like those chapters, the movements of a piece contribute in some way—sometimes very explicitly, usually more subtly—to the cohesiveness of the work.

The term derives from the practice of a composer placing a tempo marking at the start of each movement, indicating how fast or slow the music should "move." Those tempo markings traditionally have been written in Italian—*allegro* for fast, *andante* for moderate speed, *adagio* for very slow, *presto* for very fast, etc. Movements are frequently identified in conversation or writings about a composition by those tempo marks—"The andante has a very dramatic character"; "The adagio is very lyrical." (Some non-Italian composers, especially since the nineteenth century and the rise of nationalism, have insisted on writing tempo markings in their own native language, but the Italian terms still remain in common use.)

A symphony typically has four movements, a concerto three. In most works with several movements, there is a clear pause between each; sometimes, as in the third and fourth movements of Beethoven's Fifth Symphony or the first and second movements of Mendelssohn's Violin Concerto, there is no break, but the delineation of the separate movements is still clear.

The idea of putting several movements together to constitute a single composition started around the fourteenth century:

Suite: At first usually written to be played on the lute, a suite consisted of a series of movements, each one based on a popular dance style of the day. By the seventeenth century, and on through at least the first half of the eighteenth, suites were written for different solo instruments or instrumental ensembles, and the dance movements became highly stylized. A typical Baroque suite—whether for solo keyboard, solo violin, solo cello, violin and keyboard, or an orchestra—would contain an allemande (an old German dance), a courante (which had French and Italian origins), a sarabande (a slow, courtly dance) and a gigue (a stylized version of the Irish or English jig). To these basic, four movements, a composer could add on others, such as the minuet or a gavotte. Notable examples of this form are Bach's English Suites for keyboard, six Cello Suites and four Orchestral Suites; and George Frideric Handel's *Water Music* Suite.

By the nineteenth century, long after the Baroque suite had been replaced by other musical forms, the term *suite* took on a new meaning. It refers most often to a sequence of movements, almost always for orchestra, fashioned out of a larger work—as in the suite from Peter Ilyich Tchaikovsky's ballet *The Nutcracker*, the two suites from Sergei Prokofiev's ballet *Romeo and Juliet*, and the two suites from Edvard Grieg's music for the play *Peer Gynt*. Occasionally a suite of excerpts will be written in one continuous movement, rather than individual ones; the suite from Richard Strauss's opera *Der Rosenkavalier* and the suite from Igor Stravinsky's ballet *The Firebird* are prime examples. In all of these cases, the suite provides the main highlights from the complete score; in the case of suites from operas, the vocal lines are given to instruments in the orchestra.

This is yet another kind of suite, one that also began to appear in the nineteenth century and beyond. It is neither based on dance forms nor made up of extracts from another work, but merely presents a number of individual movements in a variety of forms, all related by mood, style, or thematic material.

Getting back to the Baroque time, the popular orchestral dance suite more or less evolved into another structure, one that would have a far more lasting impact:

Symphony: Since the middle of the eighteenth century, when the symphony was perfected by Haydn, this particular structure has been one of the most important in classical music, providing a substantial outlet for a composer's creativity and a challenge to an orchestra's talents. A symphony can be abstract, in the sense of representing nothing but pure musical thought (symphonies by Haydn, Mozart, Franz Schubert, and Johannes Brahms are among those that fit this description). A symphony can be a means for making a philosophical or intensely dramatic statement, like the Third, Fifth, and Ninth of Beethoven, where the notes seem to many listeners to be infused with extra-musical significance. A symphony can be very specific, as in the case of Hector Berlioz's *Symphonie fantastique*, describing certain events or feelings. A symphony can aim to encompass the full spectrum of human emotion and aspiration, as in the works of Gustav Mahler.

Certain traditions, passed along for centuries, help to define the symphonic form. The first movement, as already discussed, is typically in "sonata form." The second movement is usually slow, perhaps reflective or lyrical, perhaps moody or dramatic. The third movement is usually a three-part form—a minuet back in the days of Haydn and Mozart, a scherzo since the days of Beethoven. (More on the minuet and scherzo in a moment.) The finale can be in any number of forms, most commonly another "sonata form" or a "rondo" (more on rondo in a moment, too).

There is considerable flexibility within this standard layout of movements. Tchaikovsky, for example, successfully broke with convention by writing a slow first movement and a slow finale for his Symphony no. 6. Since the first movement is slow, the second is faster, in this case a would-be waltz, with five beats to the bar instead of three. And the third movement is a propulsive march, instead of a scherzo. Mahler likewise experimented with ways of building a symphony, often adding extra movements.

However conceived, a symphony is, like a large novel, a substantial document, one with an abundance of ideas and arguments and emotions, brought together into a logical, coherent, communicative statement.

One of the traditional movements of a symphony—as well as a solo sonata, a string quartet, and other works—that is particularly logical in construction has had two names over time:

Minuet and Scherzo: Perhaps the easiest form in classical music to grasp is one that had its start in a popular dance of the seventeenth century called the minuet. Its rhythm—three beats to the bar—and its rather courtly air attracted Baroque composers, who frequently used minuets in multiple-movement works. By the time Bach was putting a minuet into a keyboard suite, no one was thinking about dancing to the music. It was just pure music. It was also a specific form.

A minuet is not complete on its own; it has a counterpart or complement. Initially, this second entity was called Minuet II, to distinguish it from Minuet I. The practice was to play Minuet I, then Minuet II, then go back and repeat Minuet I. Voila! A three-part, symmetrical structure. Eventually, a new term was applied to Minuet II, reflecting the way that composers orchestrated it. It was common to provide contrast in that second minuet by having only three instruments, usually woodwinds, play it; this led to the term *trio* to describe Minuet II. In time, it made no difference how many instruments played that second dance; the "trio" label stuck. Think of a pair of bookends; they represent the minuet. The book in between is the trio.

As styles changed, and the Classical era followed the Baroque, the minuet and trio became a standard feature of symphonies and other multiple-movement works. It was usually placed as the third movement out of four. Mozart and Haydn, in particular, emphasized the contrast between the minuet and trio by coloring the orchestration of the trio with lots of woodwinds, often giving it a rustic flavor. Then along came Beethoven. The minuet seemed a little too draggy and old-fashioned to him, so he revved up the engine and slapped a new name on the form—*scherzo*, which means "joke" in Italian. The result was not necessarily funny, but certainly more dynamic in outline and usually faster, too. A scherzo still has a contrasting section in the middle that is called a trio.

This new form became the norm after Beethoven. Composers writing string quartets or sonatas or symphonies included a scherzo movement as a rule. The character of a scherzo can vary widely and wildly, from the thundering scherzos in Anton Bruckner's symphonies, to the fantastical or nostalgic ones in those by Mahler, to the frightening one in John Corigliano's Symphony no. 1. Composers do not always follow the old structural model, as in the case of that Corigliano work. But a scherzo will invariably have a strong rhythmic edge (a reminder that the form was originally a dance) and lots of character and color (thanks to Beethoven). Some composers spice things up by having more than one trio, creating a larger movement in the process.

Incidentally, there's no need to say "minuet and trio" or "scherzo and trio" when referring to this form; the "trio" is understood to be a component part of either a "minuet" or "scherzo."

Classical composers very much like the idea of bringing back musical material. You see this in sonata form in the recapitulation. You also see it in a minuet or scherzo, where the whole first section returns after the trio. There's another structure that involves this satisfying symmetry:

Rondo: This popular form turns up often either as a movement (usually the finale) of a multiple-movement work or as a stand-alone piece (often for keyboard). Although composers try lots of different approaches, the basic outline of a rondo is always clear. There is an opening section of music that provides the central reference point. After it is played, new material is introduced, followed by a return to the opening material. Then, yet another episode of new material is introduced, followed by yet another return to the opening. And so on. That opening music just keeps coming around, providing the unity for the composition.

A well-known, delightful example of a rondo is the spirited finale to Mozart's Piano Sonata in A Major, K. 331, called *Rondo alla Turca* (the music has characteristics that eighteenth-century listeners thought sounded Turkish). Rondos turn up frequently in piano concertos, too, again typically as finales.

By the way, just to make things more complicated, there's a combination of sonata form and rondo, usually shortened to sonata-rondo or rondo-finale. (Mahler had a particular talent for this hybrid form.) In brief, the music acts mostly like a rondo, except that there is at some point a development section—like in a sonata form. No need to worry about the distinctions, though. It's just interesting to note the variety of structural options available to composers. A perennial favorite among those options is one that is readily grasped, especially by jazz fans:

Theme and Variations: Think of a jazz band playing an old stan-dard, say, *Green Dolphin Street*. The ensemble plays the tune through once straight, then puts it through a series of impro-visations. This, in essence, is what happens in the classical struc-ture called theme and variations. The composer first lays out a theme, a clear-cut melody supported by harmonic progressions underneath. After that, any number of variations on that theme are presented, each one exploring a different aspect of the mel-ody or perhaps concentrating on the harmony, or maybe even just the rhythmic outline of the melody.

The variations typically get more and more complex and brilliant; it can become very difficult to recognize the original theme when things get too fancy. As a rule, the theme will return at some point before the end of the piece, sometimes note-for-note as it was played at the beginning (Bach's *Goldberg* Variations is an example) or sometimes given a little final em-bellishment.

Theme and variations can be a stand-alone composition (such as Brahms's *Variations on a Theme by Haydn* or Sergei Rach-maninoff's *Rhapsody on a Theme of Paganini*), or serve as a movement within a multiple-movement work, like a symphony, concerto, sonata, or string quartet (such as the fourth and final movement of Beethoven's Symphony no. 3). In either case, the composer's goal is to demonstrate as much inventiveness as pos-sible, finding myriad ways of transforming the theme with each Variation, yet making all of the variations add up to a cohesive, satisfying musical statement.

Theme and variations, rondo, scherzo, and sonata form—all of these are among the building blocks a classical composer can employ in the building of a composition, large or small. The symphony is one of the grandest of those compositions, with its individual movements integrated into an overall design, one big thought involving an ensemble of musicians all working together in a common cause. It's the same in a string quartet or piano trio, works that normally have the same number of movements of a symphony and aim for the same breadth of concept—a group of players unified, playing as one.

Individuality is also very much a part of classical music, of course. There's the solo sonata—a sonata by Bach for solo violin, a piano sonata by Beethoven for piano. You can't get more alone than that. For a long time, a sonata for solo instrument and piano was also considered more of an individual than a dual effort; one part or the other would be decidedly in the spotlight.

By the time Beethoven started turning out sonatas for two instruments, there was no question of anyone hogging the attention; he wrote for two equal partners. That's also how he and many composers have treated another great multimovement structure:

Concerto: In its most common usage, a concerto is a work for solo instrument and orchestra, usually in three movements. The concerto emerged out of a tradition of the 1600s called "concerto grosso"—a work that pitted a small instrumental ensemble against a larger one. By 1700, composers became more interested in the idea of a single instrument interacting with an orchestra, coinciding with the arrival of more and more virtuoso musicians. The Baroque era saw hundreds of such concertos (Antonio Vivaldi alone composed more than four hundred of them).

A Baroque concerto typically has three movements that follow a set pattern of tempos—fast, slow, fast. The melodic material in each movement is derived from one theme, tossed back and forth in a variety of ways between soloist and ensemble, with a great deal of melodic manipulation, harmonic development, and often considerable variety of tone coloring. As a rule, the orchestra is made up only of string instruments in Baroque concertos.

In the Classical era, the concerto evolved into an increasingly sophisticated and colorful, even dramatic, form. The orchestra was expanded to include wind instruments and sometimes timpani. The three-movement form was still the norm. The first movement expands upon the principles of sonata form, with contrasting themes, an extended development of those themes, and a recapitulation of the themes. The composer can give all the themes to the orchestra at the outset, then let the soloist come in to repeat and begin developing them; the soloist may also enter with brand-new themes to thicken the plot. Toward the end of the movement, there is a cadenza for the soloist. It is invariably launched in the same way—the orchestra reaches an expectant chord and stops playing; the soloist then offers a fanciful elaboration on all of the melodic material in the movement. In many cases, cadenzas would be improvised on the spot; in other cases, they would be written out beforehand, either by the soloist or the composer (often one and the same). There might also be a cadenza in the remaining movements. Mozart was the supreme composer of concertos in this period; his nearly two dozen piano concertos rank among his most inspired creations, offering a wealth of melodic interest, instrumental coloring, wit, eloquence, and even profundity.

Beethoven expanded on the concerto model left by Mozart; his Violin Concerto and five piano concertos were longer and more involved than any beforehand. They came closer to the weight and breadth of a symphony; Piano Concerto no. 5, nicknamed the *Emperor*, has much the same nobility of spirit as his Symphony no. 3, called the *Eroica* ("Heroic").

Concertos continued to expand in terms of length and content in the nineteenth century. Since the twentieth century, composers have followed all sorts of models—the tight integration of a Baroque concerto; the gentlemanly argument of soloist and orchestra in a Mozart concerto; and the dramatic confrontation between two powerful protagonists in Beethoven and Brahms.

Some concertos are clearly intended as little more than a display vehicle for the soloist, but, more often, are devised as dialogues. The Beethoven style of opposing forces is particularly expressive and arresting; in the slow movement of his Piano Concerto no. 4, you can actually hear a contest of wills as an angry orchestra is slowly, steadily subdued by the piano's persistently calm, tender music. The soaring piano concertos of Tchaikovsky and Rachmaninoff present such tight fusions between the two forces that melodic lines become doubly intense.

The twentieth century saw another type of concerto occasionally—one without a soloist. Bártok's *Concerto for Orchestra* is the most famous example. Here, each section of the orchestra—strings, woodwinds, brass, and percussion—is given opportunities to shine in a large-scale work.

Composers have long had other structural outlets for writing orchestral pieces. One of the first came from opera:

Overture or Prelude: In its most common usage, this is a single-movement, musical form meant to precede something—usually an opera. As such, it may contain music to be heard later in that opera, or it may merely serve up a sense of what's in store onstage. It is not uncommon for a composer to use good old sonata form as a means of organizing the material in an overture. The best overtures are notable for their content as well as structure, and are frequently played in concerts out of the original context. The overtures to Mozart's *The Marriage of Figaro* and Rossini's *The Barber of Seville* are but two popular examples.

A term often used instead of *overture* is *prelude*, such as Wagner's Prelude to *Tristan und Isolde*. Such works may differ from an overture in that there is no clear-cut ending; instead, the music of the prelude flows directly into the opera.

Occasionally, you will come across a work called a prelude that isn't from an opera, which never was intended to have an introductory function, but is a stand-alone piece. This kind of prelude is usually for keyboard or other solo instrument, and can be in a very free form. In the Baroque era, it was common for composers to write a particular pair of pieces in the same key—a prelude and fugue. Chopin established the idea of a prelude that needed no fugal counterpart; other composers, such as Rachmaninoff, also wrote independent pieces in a variety of forms and moods called preludes.

Likewise, there is a kind of overture that does not set up an opera or other stage work, but exists entirely on its own. These overtures typically seek to capture the essence of a literary work, historic event, or aspect of nature. Berlioz's *Le corsaire* Overture is such a piece. But there is a much more frequently encountered example of this descriptive musical form:

Tone Poem or Symphonic Poem: These terms, used more or less interchangeably, describe a specific type of program music—music that attempts to depict something nonmusical, like a poem, a painting, a historical or fictional character or event, etc. A tone poem is an orchestral work, usually in one movement. The concept was developed with particular flair in the mid-nineteenth century by Franz Liszt and brought to a peak of inventiveness toward the end of that century by Richard Strauss. The latter's *Till Eulenspiegel's Merry Pranks*, based on a German folk hero, and *Also Sprach Zarathustra*, based on a book by Frederick Nietzsche, are just two examples. Mussorgsky's *Pictures at an Exhibition*, inspired by the paintings of Victor Hartmann, is a series of tone poems, each putting into music one of the artist's images.

The Vocal Side

So far, we've concentrated on forms from the perspective of instrumental music. The vocal side of music is no less interested in structural solidity and cohesive unity. Composers have used such forms as the fugue when writing for voices; the three-part form of the minuet also has a kind of counterpart in vocal music with the da capo aria, which has a middle section surrounded by two identical components. And, as in instrumental music, there are both large and small structures that have attracted composers over the centuries. Two of the earliest and most impressive are somewhat related:

Cantata: Starting in the seventeenth century, the cantata emerged as a potent musical form, employing a solo singer or singers and orchestra; a chorus might be included as well. The text can be either religious or secular. Typically, a cantata of the Baroque period consists of a series of separate movements—arias for solo voice, choruses for the choir—made into a cohesive whole by the words and the overall atmosphere of the music. Of the cantatas with religious texts, none are more valued than the two hundred–plus by Bach, composed for Lutheran church services. Cantatas continued to be written after the Baroque period, but not in nearly the same numbers. A twentieth-century example is *Alexander Nevsky* by Sergei Prokofiev, which contains solo, choral, and purely orchestral movements adapted from his score for the epic Sergei Eisenstein film of that name.

Sharing some of the characteristics of a cantata is another large-scale strucure made up of several movements:

Oratorio: Where a cantata can be written for just one singer and can have a sacred or secular text, an oratorio calls for a chorus, as well as solo singers, and is based on a religious text that, most often, has a dramatic narrative or deeply contemplative character.

The oratorio began to flourish in the seventeenth century and reached its pinnacle when Handel produced a series of masterpieces during the next century. Most of his oratorios were based on the Old Testament, to be performed during the Lenten season as an alternative to opera—opera houses were officially closed at that time of year. The typical Handel oratorio tells a story, with pauses for reflection in the form of arias for soloists or choral numbers. Some of his oratorios are like unstaged operas, with clearly delineated characters who get solo arias; the vivid orchestration and strong plot add to the sense of operatic weight. But Handel's most popular oratorio, *Messiah*, contains only a small dose of narrative; the bulk of the score is a contemplation on Jesus and faith.

By virtue of text, musical variety and sheer length, the oratorio clearly is a major form of classical music. Composers after the Baroque era did not turn to oratorio often, but some of those who did generated impressive results—Mendelssohn's

Elijah and Elgar's *The Dream of Gerontius* are two outstanding examples.

With religion such an integral part of human history, and music such an integral part of religion, a vast body of vocal music has accumulated over the centuries. Much of it has entered the classical repertoire, performed as concert works now, appreciated for the beauty of inspiration and integrity of structure. No religious litmus test is necessary to become familiar with the basics of sacred music, starting with the most prevalent:

Mass: From the earliest days of the Christian church, portions of the Latin Mass were sung during the service. Gregorian chant is an ancient example. Each stylistic period in music history has included major composers writing Masses for chorus a cappella or with accompaniment. By the 1600s, certain traditions were established, including the six parts of the Mass to be set to music—these are the *Kyrie, Gloria, Credo, Sanctus, Benedictus,* and *Agnus Dei.* In addition to chorus and orchestra (and often organ), a Mass often calls for solo singers as well.

More often than not, the texts of the Mass help define the music. The *Kyrie,* for example, has three lines; the first and third are the same. For a composer, that's an easy invitation to use a three-part form for that part of the piece. The *Agnus Dei* is in three lines, the first two the same; the music may well follow the same pattern. The *Sanctus* and *Benedictus* both end with the same words, so, again, the music for those words is likely to be the same.

Composers have followed many other traditions over the ages. The opening line of the *Gloria*—"Glory to God on the highest"—generally gets a lively treatment, with the melody taking the voices upward. The next line—"And on earth, peace"—usually brings those voices down to much lower pitches and the mood of the music abruptly switches to one of calm. Such descriptive devices can be found in Mass after Mass; the best composers find fresh and telling ways of conveying the words and messages of the liturgy.

Among the most inspired Mass composers are Haydn, Mozart, Beethoven, and Schubert. But looming over them all is the non-Catholic Bach. His sublime B-minor Mass was never intended for a service, but rather as a culmination of all that he had learned about writing a Mass; it ranks among the monuments of Baroque musical art. For a completely original take on the Mass as musical form, there is Leonard Bernstein's ambitious "theater piece" for singers, dancers, and orchestra called simply *Mass*. It incorporates almost all of the text of the Latin Mass, interspersed with other music; a crisis of faith by the celebrant of the Mass provides the dramatic climax of the piece.

A specific type of Mass, one offered for the repose of souls, also generated a specific musical form:

Requiem: As with an everyday Mass, portions of the Latin Mass for the Dead have been frequently set to music since ancient times. Traditionally, several texts are used, making a requiem longer than a regular Mass. Among the standard texts are: *Introit, Kyrie, Dies Irae, Offertorio, Sanctus, Benedictus, Agnus Dei, Lux Aeterna*, and *Libera me* (this last item is from the Latin burial service). Solo voices and chorus are usually employed, dividing up certain portions of the texts and sharing others.

Of the texts, particular attention has been paid by composers to the long *Dies Irae* ("The Day of Wrath") passage, with its imagery of the last trumpet call to judgment and the threat of fire and brimstone. The obvious dramatic nature of the words has inspired some hair-raising music, notably in the requiems by Hector Berlioz and Giuseppe Verdi. As in the regular Mass, the words themselves often spark the music, but there has been a considerable variety of approaches to the same words. There also have been certain traditions over the ages. One of them comes in the *Offertorio*, when the text refers to the seed of Abraham. Composers frequently use imitative counterpoint for this line about procreation; each new entrance of the theme suggests a new generation. This passage in Verdi's Requiem, sung by four soloists, is a fine example; nearly a century later, Benjamin Britten achieves a striking effect by setting the same words to a fugue for chorus in his *War Requiem*.

Occasionally, composers have deliberately tried to soften the most unsettling side of the Mass for the Dead; Gabriel Fauré's Requiem excludes the *Dies Irae* entirely, and is written in a style that comforts rather than confronts. (Also soothing, but unrelated to the traditional Latin Requiem, is Brahms's *A German Requiem*, a memorial work that uses biblical passages he chose himself.)

Bach never wrote a requiem, but he did address a particular death in another imposing musical form:

Passion: This is a type of oratorio for solo singers, chorus, and orchestra. The text is drawn primarily from one of the four gospels and deals with the arrest, suffering, and death of Jesus. Originally, Passions were performed on Palm Sunday and/or Good Friday as part of a service. Some Passions confine themselves solely to a gospel text, but the most famous examples of this genre are by Bach, who followed a German-Lutheran tradition of weaving nonbiblical, contemplative texts into the piece. Some of these other texts would be used for arias to be sung by a soloist; others would serve as hymns to be sung by the chorus and/or congregation.

Bach's two extant works in this form, the *St. John Passion* and, especially, *St. Matthew Passion*, have established themselves outside of religious contexts and are frequently performed as concert works. The brilliance of Bach's vocal and instrumental writing, as well as his sense of how to intensify the dramatic events described in the text, help these works to transcend denominational considerations. Although a few composers since Bach's time have written Passions, none have gained a similar foothold in the repertoire. But an intriguing, nonclassical attempt at writing a modern Passion was made in 1970 by a composer who went on to much more lucrative projects—Andrew Lloyd Webber. His *Jesus Christ Superstar* (with an adaptation of gospel texts by Tim Rice) follows, in many ways, the tradition so profoundly perfected by Bach.

In Performance

Classical music can be appreciated by anyone who takes the time to listen, but it can only be realized effectively in performance by well-trained musicians. There is an art to performing, as there is to composing.

For those just beginning to experience classical music, the specialized aspects of the actual music making may seem a little mysterious, even strange—not to mention awfully formal—especially in live concerts. All those white ties and tails, all those serious expressions, all those rules about when to applaud. But classical musicians really are just ordinary people (well, maybe not all of them), and the concertgoing experience isn't as intimidating as it may look. It's easy to get a handle on what is going on up there onstage.

In the case of a recital, the situation is particularly simple. The musician giving the recital is in complete charge of what is played and how. It's interesting to note that the recital—a concert for a solo musician, such as a pianist, or a soloist with accompanist, such as a violinist and pianist—only emerged in the early decades of the nineteenth century. Before that, the idea of a single person giving a public performance for a couple of hours would have been considered almost bizarre, certainly indulgent. Even Niccolo Paganini, the sensational violin virtuoso, shared his concerts with an orchestra or other ensembles and maybe a singer or two. Liszt, who possessed phenomenal pianistic skills and an ego to match, is usually credited with the first significant, all-solo concerts, and the first use of the term *recital* to describe them. Recitals remain a part of concert life and provide a valuable opportunity to gauge a soloist's talents.

A chamber-music program presents a small group of musicians who are, in essence, playing and thinking as one. In a string quartet, the first violinist—the one sitting closest to the edge of the stage to the audience's left—usually has the most important melodic part in the music. But that does not necessarily make the player more important than the other three. During rehearsals, each member of the quartet is likely to have an equal voice in deciding on repertoire and matters of interpretation. Democratic principles generally hold sway. Not so in the largest contingent of classical musicians:

Orchestra: The first orchestras were formed specifically to provide the instrumental support for operas around 1600, but independent ensembles put together for the purpose of playing purely orchestral music soon appeared. The makeup of these ensembles went through various changes over the decades as instruments were invented or improved, but by the late-eighteenth century, the basic components of the present-day orchestra were firmly in place: strings, woodwinds, brass, and percussion.

There are four principal string instruments, in descending order of pitch: violin, viola, cello (also called violoncello), and double bass (often called just "bass"). The violin as we know it today emerged around 1500, the viola and cello a few decades later, the double bass by 1600. Various changes in the making of these instruments over the centuries resulted in gradually increasing volume and resonance. An orchestra will typically have two sections of violins (called first violins and second violins), one section of violas, one section of cellos, and one section of basses.

Woodwind instruments are so called primarily because most of them were originally made of wood. In addition to the flute and its smaller, high-pitched cousin the piccolo, the other major woodwind instruments are the oboe, clarinet, and bassoon. Many orchestras also add an English horn, which isn't really English or a horn, for that matter, but a darker-toned cousin to the oboe; and a contrabassoon, which has lower notes than a bassoon. A few composers have added another woodwind to the mix—the saxophone, which started out as a classical instrument but, by the twentieth century, enjoyed its greatest use in jazz and pop music.

The brass family of instruments contains trumpet, trombone, horn (commonly called French horn, because the horn as we know it today first emerged in that country), and the low-note-emitting tuba.

The percussion section of an orchestra typically contains timpani (sometimes called kettle drums, on account of their shape), bass drum (a very large drum placed in a vertical position), and cymbals. Added to this mix may be a snare drum (a small drum of the sort commonly used in dance bands), triangle (a small, metal instrument in a triangular shape that emits a high-pitched ring when struck), xylophone (a set of wooden slats, arranged like a keyboard, struck with wooden beaters, producing pitched tones from resonating tubes underneath the slats), and bells. Also found in some percussion sections are the piano and celesta (a small, pianolike instrument with a soft metallic sound made popular by the *Dance of the Sugar-Plum Fairy* in Tchaikovsky's ballet *The Nutcracker*).

The size of orchestras continually evolved, from relatively modest groupings of a couple dozen players in the seventeenth century to the standard full orchestra size today, which is around one hundred players. About sixty of those players will be strings. Different seating placements have been fashionable at different times. The most common arrangement seen onstage today is for the strings to be arranged in a semicircle around the conductor, with the first and second violins starting on the left, violas and cellos following around the curve to the right; the basses will be behind the cellos or another section of the orchestra. The woodwind section is usually placed in the center of the stage, the brass section usually toward the rear behind the woodwinds and/or along the side, behind one of the string sections. The percussion section will be somewhere along the back of the orchestra.

In a concert hall, one member out of the hundred or so of an orchestra will get applause merely for walking onstage:

Concertmaster: The head of the violin section, who sits in the first row (or "stand") of violins, just to the left of the conductor on the outside, closest to the rim of the stage, is designated the "concertmaster." Because so much of an orchestra's quality of sound depends on the violins, which play the lion's share of melodic lines in a composition, the concertmaster must be an exceptional player, technically and artistically (many compositions have passages for solo violin, which the concertmaster will be called on to perform). This is considered to be the most important job in an orchestra, serving as the ensemble's front man (or woman). Conductors routinely rely on concertmasters to help decide how the violin section should approach a phrase technically and how best to achieve a certain tone.

By tradition, the concertmaster is the last member of the orchestra to arrive onstage before a concert begins (and, also by tradition, is applauded). He or she will signal to the principal oboe player to sound an A—the note that all of the musicians will tune their instruments to, often one section at a time (all the woodwinds, all the brass, then all the strings). When the tuning is done, the concertmaster will sit down, which is the signal for the conductor to come onstage and start the performance.

This is but one of the venerable traditions surrounding orchestras. In the early days of orchestras, there was another, uncomfortable one—the players used to stand during performances (except the cellists, who have no choice but to sit while playing). This practice died out during the nineteenth century. Also during that century, a conventional dress code emerged— the same formal dress of men in high society at that time, white tie and tails. (Women weren't generally admitted into orchestras until the twentieth century, so their dress code wasn't an issue; today, they typically wear their choice of black clothes.) Although occasional efforts have been made to loosen these restrictions, most orchestras continue to follow them, providing a sense of historic continuity and tradition. Exceptions are pops concerts or special events, when contemporary formal wear—black tie for the men—or maybe white jackets will be worn.

Formalities also tend to be observed by the smaller version of an orchestra:

Chamber Orchestra: This type of ensemble usually reflects the typical size of those in the days of Handel, Haydn, and Mozart, when performance venues tended to be on the intimate side. The total number of players is generally from about twenty-five to forty, with the same mix of strings, woodwinds, and brass as the full-size variety. The repertoire for such groups is geared toward the eighteenth and early-nineteenth centuries, but there is also a fair amount of music from more recent times written specifically for chamber orchestra.

Until about the last third of the twentieth century, few people gave much thought to the fact that a lot of music played by full-size or chamber-size orchestras was originally written for very different instruments:

Period Instruments: Also described as "original instruments," this term refers to instruments that are either authentic to the time of the composition being played or reproductions of them. This has been a painstaking effort on the part of several scholars to re-create the actual sonic experience of audiences in the sixteenth, seventeenth, eighteenth, and early-nineteenth centuries—an effort labeled the "authenticity movement." This has resulted in a fascinating proliferation of ensembles consisting of period instruments that offer "historically informed performances."

Instead of modern violins fitted with wire strings, early violin models with lamb-gut strings are used; the result is a softer, subtler sound. The bows, too, revert to the slightly smaller variety used in past centuries. Wooden flutes replace contemporary metal ones. Valveless horns and trumpets, rather than present-day valved instruments, also will be played. If a keyboard instrument is called for, it will be a harpsichord or the precursor to the modern piano, the smaller, thin-sounding fortepiano.

Although it is not easy for contemporary musicians to master these old instruments (especially those valveless brass ones) and authentic styles of playing on them, much progress has been made since the nearly seismic stirrings of the authenticity movement in the 1970s, when out-of-tune playing was, sadly, far from uncommon. Such ensembles as the Orchestre Romantique et Revolutionnaire and the Hanover Band are among the most successful at providing not just a history lesson, but an impressive demonstration of music making. Leading conductors of period instrument ensembles include John Eliot Gardiner, Christopher Hogwood, and Roger Norrington. Music by Bach, Handel, Haydn, Mozart, Beethoven, and Schumann has been widely recorded using period instruments, providing an extraordinary opportunity to rethink and rehear familiar works.

One of the most beneficial aspects of the authenticity movement has been to encourage conductors of regular, modern-instrument orchestras to adopt some of the performance practices of the period-instrument groups. These especially include leaner textures (achieved partly by using fewer strings and partly by having them play without vibrato, as the earlier strings commonly did) and swifter tempos.

Deciding such matters is but one responsibility of the person who stands on the podium and faces an orchestra:

Conductor: As instrumental ensembles got larger in the seventeenth century, the need for someone to lead them in performance became more pressing. At the very least, someone had to be responsible for getting the music started by signaling the first beat, and making sure that the music ended when it was supposed to. Initially, ensembles took these cues from a musician within the group. This was usually the leader of the violin section or the keyboard player (a harpsichord and subsequent keyboard instruments were commonly used in large instrumental groups from Bach's time up to Beethoven's).

Gradually, the idea of having a conductor—someone whose only function was to guide the rehearsals and the performances—took hold. At first, the principal duties were to establish a tempo and keep everyone on track as the music progressed, to make sure that everyone was playing the right notes and following other indications provided by the composer in the score—how loud or soft to play a particular passage, for example. Soon, the conductor did much more than look after such purely technical details; the job entailed deciding on an overall approach to a composition and getting all of the players to go along with it.

It has always been possible for small- or medium-size ensembles to do without a conductor, especially if performing music that has little rhythmic complexity. The Orpheus Chamber Orchestra, for example, has enjoyed remarkable success as a conductorless organization since being founded in 1972. The musicians decide in a democratic fashion on tempos and phrasing during rehearsals. But this is not a common occurrence.

Most orchestras, large and small, continue to want and need a leader on the podium who, for better or worse, sets the parameters for making music. What we hear in performance is, to a great extent, determined by the conductor, not the individual players.

Things can get a little complicated when an orchestra programs a concerto. The soloist in that concerto will bring his or her own ideas about the piece to the rehearsal, while the conductor may arrive with other ideas. Compromise, sometimes after intense struggle, will be necessary if the performance is to have cohesion. The conductor has to be able to anticipate and respond to what the soloist is doing, so that the orchestra will make its contributions in synch. (On one unusual occasion, conductor Leonard Bernstein announced to the audience before a performance that he did not agree with the tempos that the evening's soloist, Glenn Gould, wanted in Brahms's Piano Concerto no. 2, but would accommodate him.)

A conductor may be hired just for a specific program ("guest conductor") or engaged as an ensemble's artistic leader—usually under the title "music director." This often entails many administrative duties, including the hiring (and firing) of players and the selection of repertoire to perform. But the most important concern for a conductor is the same as for a solo musician:

Interpretation: A piece of music is almost always very specific, not just in terms of the actual notes on the page, but the instructions on how fast or slow, how loud or soft, how sweet or dramatic, to play them. But this does not mean that every performance of that piece will sound the same. Ideally, no two performances of a piece ever sound the same. That's because of interpretation.

Every musician brings his or her own ideas and talents to a composition, so the results can be as varied and unique as fingerprints. Classical music is like perpetually wet clay. A musician grabs hold of it and molds it according to personal tastes and experiences, leaving an imprint on the music. But it's never a permanent imprint; the next musician to come along can smooth out the clay and mold it in a completely different way. Obviously, this sort of freedom can be abused. A musician who has not researched the composer and the composition sufficiently may make decisions about tempos or phrasing that are stylistically inappropriate, even detrimental to the piece. But there are relatively few absolutes in music. There is always room for new approaches.

You can get a good idea of the variety of interpretations by checking out a dozen recordings of a very familiar work like Beethoven's Fifth Symphony, a representative sampling from the last seventy years or so, or even just the last twenty-five. Listen to the way each conductor takes just the first couple of measures of the opening movement—the famous da-da-da-dum, da-da-da-dum. You'll be amazed how different each one sounds in terms of speed, articulation, and emphasis. It's the same with most works of music, from a piano sonata to an oratorio to a string quartet. This element of individuality is part of the fun of exploring classical music. Curious Listeners who seek exposure to different interpretations can greatly enhance their own appreciation of the music in the process, refining their own preferences and setting fresh expectations.

The face in a portrait painting cannot be altered; the figure carved in marble cannot be made to change positions. But classical music is not frozen, in time or place. Once composed, it is not finished. It has only just begun to live.

FIVE

The Composers

The history of classical music is as much a history of persons as it is of concepts and forms. Each era, from the Middle Ages on, has produced an enormous number of remarkable figures with singular talents for composing. The biographies of the truly great could fill many books, so this is just a very subjective sampling of fifty-one men and women who have made notable contributions.

In the alphabetical list that follows, you'll find basic biographical information and a sense of what makes each individual significant; representative works are mentioned for each to provide an initial avenue for exploring more deeply.

John Adams (b. 1947): He started composing at ten in his native Massachusetts and later studied with some of America's leading composers. After moving to San Francisco in 1971, he began to make waves with his individualistic version of the style known as minimalism. Perhaps his greatest fame came in the opera house, especially with *Nixon in China*, but his instrumental works have enjoyed great success as well. His early, heavily minimalistic pieces, such as *Shaker Loops* for strings and *Short Ride in a Fast Machine* for orchestra, reveal tremendous energy.

In the 1980s, a deeper, more complex style emerged in such works as *Harmonielehre*, with its mystical and psychological overtones. The 1990s saw a continual evolution of the Adams sound—intricate, alternately lyrical and kinetic, with vibrant instrumental coloring. The Violin Concerto and *Century Rolls* for piano and orchestra are among his recent, and effective, efforts.

Johann Sebastian Bach (1685–1750): He came from a long line of German musicians, and spawned a long line, too (four of his twenty-one children became notable composers). Although he never traveled beyond his own country and spent his entire musical life closely connected to churches, Bach influenced the entire history of Western music.

He was the supreme master of counterpoint. His genius can be heard in virtually everything he wrote; the logical progression of his musical ideas and the inventive ways he could develop each component of a theme continue to awe listeners today. Bach earned respect as an organist, though he sometimes played a little too colorfully to suit the congregation.

His longest job was as "cantor" of the city of Leipzig, which required him to teach, compose fresh music for each week's church services, and perform some menial tasks. He produced a steady stream of important choral works—dozens of cantatas, the *St. Matthew Passion*, the B-minor Mass, and many others. His *Brandenburg* Concertos, written for a variety of instrumental ensembles; *The Well-Tempered Clavier*, a series of preludes and fugues for keyboard; the *Goldberg* Variations, also for keyboard; and Concerto for Two Violins are just a few of his enduring instrumental pieces.

His final effort was a definitive examination of one of his favorite musical forms—*The Art of the Fugue*. He didn't complete the project before he died; the last fugue he was working on had a theme of four notes, which, in German musical notation, spell out B-A-C-H.

Béla Bártok (1881–1945): With a keen interest in the folk music of his native Hungary and an original sense of harmony, rhythm, and tone coloring, Bártok made some of the most significant contributions to music in the twentieth century. A superb pianist, he wrote and performed keyboard works that featured very spicy chords and percussive effects. Early on, he developed an affinity for the string-quartet form, and eventually produced six compelling works in that medium, filled with provocative sounds (eerie slithering across the strings, for example), and unusual structural designs.

The String Quartet no. 4 typifies Bártok's genius; its five movements form a symmetrical arch, with the first and fifth, second and fourth built of similar materials. The composer also is known for his distinctive kind of "night music," sounds that conjure up a mysterious moonlit world; a movement in his dazzling *Music for Strings, Percussion, and Celesta* contains a memorable example.

Brilliant instrumentation was a Bártok specialty, nowhere more compelling than in the tautly integrated Sonata for Two Pianos and Percussion. Although the public had trouble digesting some of Bártok's music, his prismatic, sometime humorous

Concerto for Orchestra, his last finished work, was an instant success.

Ludwig van Beethoven (1770–1827): Beethoven was, in many ways, a bridge between the purity and balance of Classicism and the emotional weight of Romanticism. He was a revolutionary in just about every sense of the word, reflecting in musical ways the political revolutions of his time. Born in Bonn, Germany, Beethoven moved to what was the cultural capital of the world, Vienna, and conquered it with his dazzling virtuosity at the piano and his often startling compositions. Even some of his earliest works have a "hey, pay attention to the new kid on the block" spirit.

The opening chords of his Symphony no. 1 in 1800 confirmed his originality by confusing the listener about the key of the piece. And that was just the beginning. The first movement of the Symphony no. 3, called the *Eroica* ("Heroic"), lasts as long as some entire Mozart symphonies; no one had ever dared to make such a long, complex musical statement. Beethoven's uncanny sense of how to develop themes, to fulfill their potential, made such innovations possible, and yielded the fate-crushing Symphony no. 5, the vividly pictorial no. 6 (*Pastoral*), and hard-driving no. 7.

He likewise shook up the conventional expectations for piano sonatas with startling flashes of drama, poetic sensibility, and passion (the *Moonlight* and *Appassionata* sonatas are but two examples). This same level of inspiration, content, and style can be found in his five piano concertos and single violin concerto.

Although suffering from deafness and the resultant depression before he turned thirty, Beethoven persevered. In his soundless world, he heard such majestic sounds as the Symphony no. 9, which introduced a chorus into a symphony for the first time (the *Ode to Joy*); the *Missa Solemnis*, a stunning, expansive treatment of the Latin text, unlike anyone else's before or since; and the late, challenging piano sonatas and string quartets, which stretch intriguingly toward new musical and spiritual horizons.

Alban Berg (1885–1935): Although he started out as a disciple of Schoenberg, his only significant teacher, Berg quickly developed a unique voice. The Austrian-born composer's embrace of Schoenberg's twelve-tone revolution never restricted his lyrical impulses. His most celebrated instrumental work, the Violin Concerto, uses twelve-tone methods to produce both atonal and tonal results. Berg's probing mind enabled him to construct an entire opera (*Wozzeck*) out of traditional musical structures—scherzo, fugue, etc.—in an atonal mode.

His *Chamber Concerto* is built essentially along mathematical lines (the number three provides the solution); the melodic material is derived entirely from the names Schoenberg, Berg, and Webern (Anton Webern was another important student of Schoenberg). And Berg's *Lyric Suite* is filled with musical codes that refer to his own extramarital affair. Such under-the-surface elements add to an appreciation of Berg's intentions, but it is what he did to reveal the communicative—almost romantic—potential of atonal music that makes him such an important figure.

Hector Berlioz (1803–1869): Like Beethoven, Berlioz was every bit the musical revolutionary. The Frenchman's first rebellion came against his parents, who wanted him to be a doctor. Berlioz bolted from medical school and entered the Paris Conservatory, where he caused no end of trouble, shaking up the traditionalists there with his super-size compositions and exceedingly novel approach to formal structure. His first major work, the *Symphonie fantastique* ("Fantastic Symphony"), was unconventional in design and content, establishing a new level of narrative "program music."

Berlioz developed the art of orchestration to its highest level to date; composers are still learning from him how to orchestrate a score. He matched the grandness of Romantic ideals with grandly scaled works—his emotion-charged Requiem, for example, called for more than two-hundred instrumentalists and an equally large chorus.

Berlioz wasn't really interested in small music; he didn't bother with piano pieces or string quartets. The orchestra was his instrument, as his rousing *Roman Carnival* and *Le corsaire* overtures and another masterful example of program music, *Harold in Italy*, amply demonstrate. His writing for voice was also special; in addition to some noble operas, he left a subtly shaded masterpiece for solo singer and orchestra, *Les Nuits d'Ete* ("Summer Nights").

Berlioz lived a life as adventurous as his music, filled with attention-grabbing antics and overwrought love affairs. (He once plotted, with almost comical results, to kill a woman who jilted him, her new husband, her mother, and then himself. He was to disguise himself as a maid to gain entry to their Paris home, carrying two pistols and, in case of misfires, vials of strychnine and laudanum. While en route from Italy to carry out this spectacular revenge, Berlioz lost his disguise and had to order another set of female servant's clothes; while waiting in Genoa for them to be made, he grew faint and fell into the sea, which helped him cool off a good deal. Eventually, he abandoned the whole scheme and moved on to other romances.) Luckily for us, Berlioz wrote deliciously about many of his experiences. He's as good a read as he is an earful.

Johannes Brahms (1833–1897): Born in Hamburg, where he earned some money playing piano in not-quite-reputable night spots, Brahms was all of twenty when he was hailed as the next great German composer by no less than Robert Schumann. By the time Brahms settled in Vienna in 1869, he had fulfilled that prediction with such imposing works as the Piano Concerto no. 1, the Piano Quintet no. 1, and *Ein Deutsches Requiem* ("A German Requiem").

Feeling the intimidating shadow of Beethoven hanging over him, Brahms procrastinated writing his first symphony; it took him fourteen years. But the struggle was worth it. With the Symphony no. 1, Brahms signaled a new kind of musical Romanticism, one with firm roots in the old Classical era that valued structure as much as content.

Brahms did not expose his heart boldly, but he didn't hide his emotions either. The combination of intellectual strength and expressive depth made him an important figure; his innate musical conservatism put him at odds with such leading figures as Franz Liszt and Richard Wagner, who were constantly stretching music in new directions.

Three more symphonies, each one superbly crafted with an ear for melodic warmth, dramatic flow, and cohesive form, added to Brahms's standing, as did the rapturous Violin Concerto and, at the end of his life, the rare autumnal beauty of his Clarinet Quintet.

Brahms didn't get along with people easily (on leaving a

party, he supposedly said, "If there's anyone here I haven't insulted, I apologize"), but his music is as approachable as it is engrossing, ennobling, and enriching.

Benjamin Britten (1913–1976): The greatest English composer of the post-war era, Britten was a precocious talent; he was composing by the age of five (some of his youthful ventures were later fashioned into one of his first notable works, *Simple Symphony*). Britten developed a particular affinity for opera and produced some of the most dramatically and psychologically potent works in that genre, but the rest of his output is no less impressive. He developed an economical style that employs a full palette of instrumental colors within a varied harmonic language that admits dissonance, without embracing atonality.

At his most direct and accessible, he could produce such brilliant works as *A Young Person's Guide to the Orchestra*, which takes a tune by England's first great composer, Henry Purcell, for a wild, eventful ride. Britten's lifelong relationship with tenor Peter Pears resulted not only in many operas, but some of the most intellectually penetrating works for solo voice in the twentieth century, such as *Serenade for Tenor Horn and Strings*. And with the *War Requiem*, Britten produced a profound musical and personal statement that revealed the full extent of his creative impulses.

Anton Bruckner (1824–1896): From a humble beginning as an Austrian schoolteacher, Bruckner slowly transformed himself into an imposing composer. After hearing the music of Wagner, he became quite energized and followed boldly down Wagner's daring harmonic path. Although he did not pursue opera,

Bruckner fashioned symphonies that seemed to breathe the same heady air as Wagnerian stage works. The enormous length and organizational structure of these symphonies caused consternation when he tried to get them performed. Gradually, their nobleness and sheer weight wore much of the opposition down.

Although still not a wildly popular composer, Bruckner enjoys a high ranking. His symphonies, notably no. 4 (*Romantic*), no. 7, and no. 8, suggest huge cathedrals, with groups of themes like grand, marble stones piled one atop the other, reaching for the sky. Bruckner died before finishing his Ninth Symphony, but its three completed movements sum up his unique combination of Romantic style and deeply spiritual thinking.

John Cage (1912–1992): The most famous member of the twentieth century's musical avant-garde, Cage gained particular notoriety for "composing" a piano piece in 1952 called "4:33"— the player is instructed to sit at the piano and play nothing for exactly four minutes and thirty-three seconds. The ambient noises in the room during that time span constitute the musical experience. Many other works likewise bent the definition of music in wild ways, but there was a genius behind such revolutionary creations.

Cage wanted people to accept music in what seemed an impossibly broad sense of the word—just about any sound. Experimentation with novel musical devices (a toy piano, for example), improvisation, chance (the notes in "Music of Changes" are determined partly by coin toss), multidisciplinary activities (combining music and film, for example), and sheer artistic anarchy were among Cage's provocative weapons in the war against conventionality.

Frederic Chopin (1810–1849): He was born in Poland, but achieved his lasting fame in Paris. He arrived there at the age of twenty, having already written two piano concertos filled with songful melodies and Polish dance rhythms that would become a major feature of his output. Chopin was a superior pianist, but an uncomfortable performer in public; he preferred private salons, where he flourished, playing mostly his own pieces. He composed almost exclusively for the piano, accumulating a large body of work that has never gone out of favor. He understood not only the piano's capacity for dramatic flourish, but also its subtlest side, unleashing nuances that no one had yet discovered.

His genuinely Romantic temperament found an eloquent outlet through his ballades, scherzos, preludes, waltzes, mazurkas, and polonaises, and established new dimensions of musical thought and structural strength. In his nocturnes, Chopin took something of the long flowing melodic lines from early nineteenth-century Italian opera, specifically the operas of Vincenzo Bellini, and fashioned refined and affecting aural poetry. A ten-year affair with the woman novelist who went by the name George Sand took a toll on Chopin's emotions and creativity; he was a broken man when it ended and died two years later, not yet forty. But he left behind uniquely beautiful music that revealed the soul of the piano.

Aaron Copland (1900–1990): Although born of Jewish-Russian heritage in New York, Copland developed an unmistakably American sound that seemed to define the Old West and vintage American values. No wonder he became the country's most beloved composer. Initially, while studying with the famed Nadia Boulanger in Paris, Copland adopted a kind of cosmopolitan, European style—abstract and bracing. But by the mid-1920s, he was beginning to develop a new voice, one that contained acerbic harmonies and some of the rhythmic punch of jazz, as in his *Piano Variations*.

Copland continued refining that sound until he reached a kind of populist approach that had strong elements of American folk music. His ballet scores *Billy the Kid, Rodeo*, and, especially, *Appalachian Spring*, reflected this unique style, which summed up the mythical ruggedness and sentiment of America. His exquisitely crafted Clarinet Concerto, commissioned by jazz great Benny Goodman, demonstrated Copland's strong lyrical gifts.

His *Fanfare for the Common Man* and *A Lincoln Portrait* (for narrator and orchestra) further demonstrated his identification with the American spirit, which wasn't enough to satisfy the notorious McCarthy Committee's communist witch-hunting in the 1950s. Copland survived that stigma and intensified his popularity with audiences. Only his experimentation with Schoenberg's twelve-tone principles during the 1960s found little favor. He stopped composing in the 1970s and concentrated on conducting and teaching.

John Corigliano (b. 1938): Son of a noted concertmaster of the New York Philharmonic (also named John Corigliano), this American composer has written some of the most accessible, and sophisticated, music of recent decades. His Clarinet Concerto and *Pied Piper Fantasy* are two examples.

Corigliano is not easily pinned down stylistically. He has used atonality at times and experimented with intriguing effects (*Chiaroscuro* for two pianos calls for one of them to be a fraction out of tune with the other). But he is also capable of intense lyricism. His wrenching Symphony no. 1, memorializing those who died from AIDS, became one of the most frequently performed new works of the past twenty-five years. His lush film score to *The Red Violin* won an Academy Award and was fashioned into a substantial violin concerto of that name.

Claude Debussy (1862–1918): One of the greatest, yet softest, revolutions in music history occurred in France as the nineteenth century was winding down. Debussy, a fine pianist who worked for a time for the same patroness who had befriended Tchaikovsky, attended the Paris World Exposition of 1889 and heard Oriental music. The sounds (particularly Javanese), the different harmonies, scales, and rhythms, caught his ear. At the same time, he found himself under the spell of daring new voices in poetry and new directions in visual art, where symbols and misty impressions took the place of heavy Romanticism or stark realism.

Out of all these influences, Debussy's unprecedented musical style as a composer evolved. It was heard in a subtly colored set of piano pieces called *Suite bergamasque*, which contains the famous, gently evocative *Clair de lune*. Even more impressive was *Prelude to the Afternoon of a Faun*, with its subtly erotic air and delicate harmonies generating a world as far removed from Beethoven or Wagner or Tchaikovsky as possible. Although Debussy loathed being called an Impressionist, no other term fits quite so well, especially when considering a work like *La Mer*, with its vibrant symphonic picture of the sea.

This apparent connection to the visual art can also be sensed in such pieces as *Nocturnes*, with their delicately applied instrumental colors; a totally original palette of musical light and shadow depicts gray clouds, bright festivals, and seductive sea nymphs under a moonlit sky. Debussy's smaller-scale music, especially the Preludes for Piano and the String Quartet, boast similar qualities. Debussy led something of a stormy love life; he drove two women, one a lover and the other his wife, to attempt suicide. But in his music, delicacy, nuance, and control prevail.

Antonín Dvořák (1841–1904): He came from a small Czech village and was expected to follow his father's trade as a butcher, but Dvořák couldn't cut it. He wanted to be a musician. And he got his way. After working as a violist in an orchestra, he concentrated on composing and got his first big break by winning a prize in Austria; one of the judges was Brahms, who helped Dvořák get a commission to write some piano duets.

These turned out to be the *Slavonic Dances*, filled with contrasts of joy and bittersweetness. Later orchestrated, they caused a sensation across Europe and launched Dvořák's career. His use of folk idioms in those dances, and many of his other works, marked him as a leading musical nationalist.

By the time he composed his shadow-tinged Symphony no. 7 and extroverted, good-natured no. 8, Dvořák was one of the most respected composers on the scene. He traveled to New York in 1891 to head the new National Conservatory of Music and absorbed many influences, notably African American spirituals and Native American folk music. His Symphony no. 9, also known as *From the New World*, managed to sound American and Slavonic simultaneously, and also revealed the composer's knack for thematic richness and structural unity.

His subsequent Cello Concerto, with its brooding passion, quickly was recognized as one of the finest such works in the repertoire. Many chamber works, especially the *American* String Quartet and *Dumky* Trio, further attest to Dvořák's melodic and expressive gifts.

Edward Elgar (1857–1934): Elgar was England's first great composer since the seventeenth century's Henry Purcell. This achievement was doubly notable considering that Elgar had no formal musical training. He taught himself most of what he knew, which was enough to attract attention as a composer with some orchestral and choral works in the 1890s.

His first masterful symphonic work, *Enigma* Variations, established him firmly as a major new voice in British music. The *Pomp and Circumstance* Marches (especially no. 1, used in many a graduation ceremony); an emotional oratorio, *The Dream of Gerontius*; two large, noble symphonies; and the poignant Violin Concerto and Cello Concerto added greatly to Elgar's fame.

Gabriel Fauré (1845–1924): Although only a rather small amount of Fauré's music is regularly performed today, the French composer made his mark with Classical refinement, melodic warmth, and a style of harmony that broke new ground. That harmonic language allowed for what had been considered dissonance previously and paved the way for the Impressionist movement in music.

Fauré's fresh sound was lighter in texture than that of predominant German composers of the time, but certainly not lighter in quality. His Requiem is a noteworthy example of this departure from tradition, avoiding the fire-and-brimstone texts usually set to music and producing instead a mood of composure, reflection, and hope. Fauré's solo-piano works and chamber music likewise abound in eloquent melody and lush harmony; his songs for voice and piano also reflect his distinctive touch (*Apres un reve* and *Lydia* are but two excellent examples).

César Franck (1822–1890): This Belgian-born composer worked as an organist for more than forty years, and also taught many young composers. His own musical works were rarely played in his lifetime and often were met with indifference, but Franck persevered. He eventually demonstrated the adage that life begins after fifty; actually, it was more like after sixty in his case.

He developed a unique style that was grounded in chromaticism—the constant shifting of harmonies. His Violin Sonata, written when he was sixty-three, demonstrated the full potency of that style. And, at sixty-six, he wrote his Symphony in D Minor, his only work in this genre; it's a superb example of "cyclical form," a piece held together by intricately recurring themes that make it seem like one long, connected thought.

George Gershwin (1898–1937): The Brooklyn-born Gershwin was not only one of the most successful composers of Tin Pan Alley and Broadway; he also played a historic role in bringing the idioms of jazz and pop into the concert hall. He started exploring the classical genre early on with a *Lullaby* for string quartet in 1920 and a one-act jazz opera *Blue Monday* two years later. In 1924, Gershwin was asked to write a work for piano and jazz orchestra for a high-profile New York concert; the result was *Rhapsody in Blue*, which caused a sensation.

He developed his craft further with such large-scale works as *Concerto in F* for piano and orchestra, the symphonic poem *An American in Paris* and, ultimately, the first great American opera, *Porgy and Bess*. Gershwin's tuneful, rhythmically vital music reverberated throughout the twentieth century, leaving its mark on many other composers.

Edvard Grieg (1843–1907): Much of classical music comes in super sizes—symphonies, concertos, and operas. Grieg, who started out as a concert pianist, developed an exceptional knack for turning out musical miniatures, notably in his collection for solo piano called *Lyric Pieces*. Many of these short works reflect influences of folk music from his native Norway; Grieg was, like Dvořák, a nationalist composer. But the "lyric" parts of those pieces—ingratiating melodies of an often sentimental shade—were also very much a part of his style.

His Piano Concerto, with its thunderous cascades up and down the keyboard and bursts of warmhearted melody, became an instant, lasting hit. His *Peer Gynt* Suites, originally composed as incidental music for the Henrik Ibsen play, still delight audiences with their atmospheric colors and infectious rhythms (*The Hall of the Mountain King* is a prime example).

George Frideric Handel (1685–1759): If his father had had his way, Handel would have become a lawyer, but the boy's musical interest would not be stifled. He managed to sneak a little keyboard instrument into the attic of the family's home in the German town of Halle, and, eventually, his father relented. Handel excelled at his musical studies and soon found work as a violinist in an opera house in Hamburg, where his first operas were produced.

He spent several years in Italy, earning fame for his operas and sacred works, then accepted a job as music director at the court of the elector of Hanover. But Handel decided to visit England first, and stayed there. His little act of unprofessionalism regarding the Hanover position might never have come back to haunt him, but the elector became the next king of England, George I. Handel had to patch things up and, in another of those irresistible legends of music history, made amends by composing the colorful orchestral work known as *Water Music.*

Handel, who spent the rest of his life in England, went on to make waves with his operas and, then, oratorios, including such imposing combinations of drama and religious reflection as *Messiah, Israel in Egypt,* and *Solomon.* With an unending source of distinctive melody and a great flair for instrumentation, Handel developed some of the most distinctive music of the Baroque era.

Joseph Haydn (1732–1809): The Austrian-born Haydn was the musical epitome of the Classical era, with its emphasis on symmetry, clarity, and elegance. He also left a lasting mark on classical music in general through his mastery of such formal structures as the symphony and string quartet. Not a bad legacy for a household servant. Haydn spent many years in uniform in the service of Prince Esterhazy, whose appetite for new music at his massive palace kept Haydn busy turning out hundreds of compositions to be performed by the court musicians.

The productivity ranged from operas, religious works, and symphonies, to pieces for the now-obscure stringed instrument called the baryton (the prince played one). Eventually, Haydn got to travel abroad, and was especially lionized in England, where he wrote the last six of his one hundred–plus symphonies. (The quantity and quality of these works earned him the nickname "Father of the Symphony.")

Back in Vienna, in his sixties, Haydn continued to compose,

hitting a fresh peak with his oratorio *The Creation*, which stands as a summation of his craft. The composer had easy command of melody, an ever-engaging way of developing themes (he could get incredible mileage out of the simplest and shortest of tunes), and a sly wit (some of Haydn's musical jokes are more readily appreciated by professional musicians, but there are plenty to amuse casual listeners).

Other representative works: Symphony no. 94 (nicknamed the *Surprise*, for a reason that becomes obvious in the second movement) and no. 104 (called the *London*), Cello Concertos, String Quartets, op. 64 and op. 76, *Mass in Time of War*, and *Lord Nelson* Mass. Incidentally, although the composer's full name is often given as Franz Joseph Haydn, scholarship indicates that he never used the name Franz.

Hildegard (of Bingen) (1098–1179): Music of the Middle Ages began to attract more attention toward the end of the twentieth century thanks to several exceptional recordings of chants that made a strong spiritual connection with many people. One of the results of this renewed interest in ancient sounds was a new focus on mystic nun and composer Hildegard.

From the age of eight, her world was a reclusive one; she was raised in a convent near the town of Bingen, in Germany, and took the veil at fifteen. In 1141, a few years after becoming an abbess, she had a vision of tongues of fire from heaven which inspired in her a rarefied flow of poetry and music. Hildegard then collected her individualistic, ethereal musical works under the title *Symphony of the Harmony of Celestial Revelations*, an unusual and moving example of early Western music.

Charles Ives (1874–1954): An audacious original, Ives got his early musical training from his father, a New England bandmaster who encouraged his son to explore unconventional sounds. That was all the encouragement Ives needed. In short order, as a teenager, he was experimenting with writing pieces in two keys simultaneously, and that's before he really got going. Ives became the first great American composer, though no one knew it until just before he died, nearly thirty years after he stopped writing music.

He consciously stayed out of musical circles after college; he went into the insurance business instead, and proved exceptionally successful at it. He composed more as a hobby, pursuing one radical path after another. Early on, in his almost normal Symphony no. 2 of 1902, he developed a signature technique of quoting from American hymns, folk songs, and patriotic tunes. He further honed that idea in such vivid orchestral works as *Central Park in the Dark* and *Three Places in New England.*

Many of his works, notably the Piano Sonata no. 2 (called the *Concord*), pose complex challenges to performers, but behind even the toughest scores is the contagious Yankee spirit of individuality that drove Ives to question every standard rule and expectation of music. He was about as far ahead of his time as he could be; the bulk of his groundbreaking work was done by 1915.

Scott Joplin (c. 1868–1917): This African American, Texas-born "King of Ragtime" craved widespread respect from the music world all his life; he finally received it six decades after his death. Not that Joplin didn't enjoy popularity in his day; his first significant piano piece, *Maple Leaf Rag*, sold more than 500,000 copies of sheet music. But he did not get to realize his greatest ambitions, especially for his full-length opera, *Treemonisha*, which wasn't staged until 1972. Today, Joplin is recognized as an extraordinary figure in America music who brought a certain sophistication to the syncopated dance form known as ragtime. His melodic flair and pianistic skill generated dozens of rags that were, in their own way, as carefully crafted and organized as waltzes by Chopin or folk-flavored dances by Brahms and Dvořák. Joplin was always concerned with how his rags were performed; the sheet music often contained a note reminding musicians that it was never right to play ragtime fast. In addition to rags, Joplin wrote elegantly syncopated waltzes, marches, songs, and the exquisitely subtle, Latin-flavored *Solace*. An unexpected Joplin revival started around 1970, resulting in astonishingly popular recordings of his music (fueled by their use in the 1974 hit movie *The Sting*) and culminating in a posthumous Pulitzer Prize for him in 1976.

Josquin (Desprez) (c. 1440–1521): Born in the Burgundy area of France, Josquin Desprez (usually referred to only by his first name) studied in Italy, where he sang in church choirs, including the pope's. By the time he returned to Burgundy in 1504, he was already an exceptionally accomplished composer of church music; his fame would spread across Europe.

Josquin made use of both counterpoint and a simpler style to produce exquisitely crafted, affecting music, with the meaning of words always coming through clearly. His settings of the Latin Mass are particularly esteemed, among them *Missa pange lingua* and *Missa l'homme arme*, and represent a pinnacle of Renaissance aural art.

Franz Liszt (1811–1886): If the Romantic era had to be defined by a single musician, it would surely be Liszt—visually, thanks to his long, flowing hair and classic profile, and artistically, thanks to unprecedented talents as a composer, pianist, and conductor. Liszt revealed the full potential of the piano, which was still a rather new instrument when he came along, and took the art of piano playing to its dizzying levels of virtuosity. His own music formed the bulk of his piano recital programs (he was the first superstar pianist); those compositions included some of the most fiendishly difficult works ever written for the piano, among them the *Transcendental Etudes*. He immortalized folk music of his native land in the popular *Hungarian Rhapsodies*.

His keyboard arrangements of other composers' works proved just as sensational with the public; when he played his transcription of Beethoven symphonies on the piano, audiences never seemed to miss the full forces of an orchestra.

Liszt, who delighted in exploring novel harmonies and musical structures, also was largely responsible for the symphonic form called a "tone poem." The *Mephisto Waltz* and *Les Preludes* are prime examples. He also demonstrated the effectiveness of thematic unity, holding long scores together by means of recurring ideas, as in his Piano Concerto no. 1 in E-flat Major and Piano Sonata in B-minor Sonata.

Women swooned over Liszt whenever he was onstage; they swooned backstage, too—he became notorious for his high-society affairs (the illegitimate daughter from one of those liaisons took up with Richard Wagner). The composer eventually took a lower form of holy orders in the Catholic Church and became the Abbe (abbot) Liszt, but, luckily for him, a vow of celibacy was not required.

Gustav Mahler (1860–1911): The Austrian-born composer famously said, "My time will come." And it did. Mahler enjoyed only intermittent success with the public during his day, but became one of the most performed and recorded composers during the past forty years. Despite a constant battle with anti-Semitism (even after, as a condition for becoming director of the Vienna Opera, he officially converted to Catholicism), Mahler carved out a celebrated career as a conductor. This security allowed him time to compose. Like Bruckner, Mahler greatly expanded the length of the traditional symphony; he also stretched Wagnerian harmony almost to the breaking point.

Mahler said that a symphony "should be like the world; it should encompass everything." He routinely put enormous contrasts into his works, often moving within a single movement between light and dark, ironic and symbolic, ethereal and banal. The force and mystery of nature figured as a prominent subject in his music, especially the First and Seventh symphonies; a longing for spiritual fulfillment propels the Second and Third.

Mahler not only called for the enormous orchestral forces, but used the instruments in novel ways, such as the double-bass solo in the First Symphony; he also introduced new sounds, such as cowbells in the Sixth. And Mahler brought voices into the symphonic picture, as Beethoven had first done. The ultimate example is his mammoth Eighth Symphony for vocal soloists, choruses, and oversize orchestra.

All of Mahler's compositions deal in some way with philosophical issues; he was forever trying to get to the truth about art, the human condition, the meaning of death, and God. His thoughts became particularly profound in *Das Lied von der Erde* ("The Song of the Earth") for two singers and orchestra. Raising weighty issues in music caused many people to misunderstand and mistrust him; the sense of self-analysis in the notes (he was one of Sigmund Freud's first patients) can still make some people uncomfortable. But Mahler touched a nerve with his music, which has been affecting many listeners ever since.

Although his greatest contribution to music was his own compositions, during his lifetime Mahler was most admired for his conducting. He still enjoys legendary status for what he achieved on the podium. He was a wild force; his balletic leaps and facial contortions while conducting made him seem like a man possessed. His demand for perfection caused many an instrumentalist and singer to despise him, but few could argue with the effectiveness of his performances. Mahler was responsible for one of the high-water marks in the artistic history of the Vienna Opera, 1899–1907, and simultaneously brought the Vienna Philharmonic to an acclaimed level. He went on to conduct several notable seasons at the Metropolitan Opera in New York and serve as music director of the New York Philharmonic.

Felix Mendelssohn (1809–1847): Born with a silver violin in his mouth, Mendelssohn never had to worry much about finances; his family in Hamburg, Germany, was in the banking business and had money as well as cultured tastes. He started to compose by the age of twelve, and at eighteen, had written his first masterpiece, a highly atmospheric overture inspired by Shakespeare's *A Midsummer Night's Dream*. Mendelssohn eventually became a conductor, too, and helped to bring the music of Bach back into the limelight.

Mendelssohn's own compositions continued apace, hitting peaks of melodic inspiration and instrumental coloring in such works as Symphony no. 3, called the *Scottish*, and Symphony no. 4, called the *Italian* (both reflect the landscapes and feelings of their namesakes). In his Violin Concerto can be heard the very essence of the early Romantic movement, with its mix of power, sentiment, and playfulness.

Other representative works: *Hebrides* Overture (also called *Fingal's Cave*), the Octet for strings, and the grand oratorio *Elijah*. Bereft over the premature death of his beloved sister, Mendelssohn himself died prematurely.

Olivier Messiaen (1908–1992): One of the most original musical voices of the twentieth century, this French composer, organist, and teacher summoned, in essence, a new dimension of time—more to the point, timelessness. Most of Messiaen's works do not move at normal speed; they unfold in a kind of suspended animation.

There is much more to the Messiaen magic than that. He also made use of Indian and Oriental harmonic languages. And he painstakingly transcribed bird songs, infusing their rhythms and the coloring of their sounds into many of his scores. Yet another influence affects virtually everything he wrote—an intense devotion to Catholicism. Messiaen sought to infuse his music with a sense of religious dogma and mystery, achieving an otherworldly sound-world.

Among his most representative efforts are *Quartet for the End of Time*, a chamber piece written and first played in the prisoner of war camp where he spent the early part of World War II; *Turangalila-symphonie*, a huge canvas of sensual sound; and *Vingt regards sur l'enfant Jesus*, a transcendental work for piano.

Wolfgang Amadeus Mozart (1756–1791): Thanks to a clever play by Peter Schaffer called *Amadeus*, and the popular film version of it, many people think of Mozart as a foulmouthed, uncouth, child of a man with a silly giggle and lots of enemies, including a rival composer who poisoned him. Well, he wasn't poisoned. And he seems to have known how to behave in society. He did enjoy scatological humor, however, but that just makes this incomparable genius more human.

Born in Salzburg and later based in Vienna, Mozart excelled in every genre he tried—opera, symphony, concerto, string quartet, piano sonata, choral music, and on down the line. Melodies came into his head so often and so quickly that he barely had time to jot them down. And he enjoyed an incredible facility for developing those melodies, carrying the listener along on an ear-spinning ride through fascinating harmonic progressions to reach uncommon peaks of expressiveness. He packed a dozen lifetimes into a single span of only thirty-five years.

Mozart started out as a child prodigy on the keyboard, a talent exploited by his father on European tours. The boy's first compositions were published when he was seven and, by the time he was a teenager, he moved a leading composer of the day, Johann Adolf Hasse, to declare: "This boy will cause us all to be forgotten." (Heard any Hasse lately?)

While under the patronage of the archbishop of Salzburg, Mozart wrote impressive symphonies, Masses, and concertos, but he really blossomed after moving to Vienna, where he lived, as he would die, beyond his means (to borrow Oscar Wilde's line). During his last years, Mozart's symphonies revealed new levels of melodic and dramatic quality; his string quartets achieved a profundity that humbled even the mighty Haydn, who had perfected the quartet form; the sophistication of his operas changed that genre forever.

Just before his death, Mozart was commissioned to write a Requiem; he didn't complete it, but what he left behind was affecting music that capped his supremely creative life. Among the other works representative of that genius are Symphony no. 40 and 41 (the *Jupiter*); Piano Concerto no. 18, 19, 20, and 21; Violin Concerto no. 5; the Clarinet Quintet; and the brief, exquisite, choral work, *Ave Verum Corpus*.

Modest Mussorgsky (1839–1881): He was the wild man of Russian music, stubbornly unconventional as a composer and very hard to get along with as a man. Mussorgsky was headed into a military career when he met influential composers of the day and decided to study music. A bad drinking habit he picked up with other soldiers stayed with him for the rest of his life; he died from alcoholism. But he left behind the most original music to come out of Russia up to that time. Mussorgsky carved out his own style of harmony, much leaner than the prevailing Romantic tastes; his chords, and even some of his melodies, seemed almost crude to listeners. Not that he had much of a public. Most of his work ended up being published after his death, and, worse yet, was routinely "revised" by well-meaning friends who softened the edges and "corrected" the harmonic weaknesses. (This was especially true of his epic opera *Boris Godunov*.)

In the twentieth century, Mussorgsky's intentions were finally honored, so audiences could appreciate fully the vitality and freshness of his artistic vision, especially in the orchestral poem *Night on Bald Mountain* and the original piano version of his descriptive masterpiece, *Pictures at an Exhibition* (more familiar in an orchestrated version of it done by Ravel).

Giovanni Pierluigi Palestrina (c. 1525–1594): Palestrina is probably the only preseventeenth-century composer routinely mentioned in the same breath as Bach and Mozart. What he achieved was, in its way, as grand and appealing as the great Renaissance cathedrals of his native Italy. Likc Josquin, he started out as a choirboy; he eventually became a member, later director, of the papal choir. By the 1550s, Palestrina was widely recognized as an exceptional composer of church music.

According to legend, when the Council of Trent tried to curb complexity in such music and return to a simpler style, Palestrina responded with his *Missa Papae Marcelli*. This choral Mass demonstrated how music could be polyphonic and still be easily absorbed, carrying its religious message directly to the faithful. The legend is not true, but this Mass, like virtually everything Palestrina wrote, really is sublime. Incidentally, on the side, the composer ran a very successful fur business.

Sergei Prokofiev (1891–1953): They called him the "enfant terrible" of Russian music, and there certainly was some truth to that. The precocious Prokofiev, who wrote his first piano pieces at five, had a rebellious streak. He found himself rather bored with the conservative principles of such teachers as Rimsky-Korsakov; at his graduation ceremony, Prokofiev shook up the establishment with a performance of his Piano Concerto no. 1, which was filled with biting sounds and audacious harmonies.

Prokofiev went on to write more and more wildly colorful, percussive music that got him charged with being a Modernist, even though he never really abandoned traditional harmony, as Schoenberg did. Even when he wasn't being provocative, as in the delightful *Classical* Symphony, a twentieth-century version of a Haydn symphony, Prokofiev was tweaking tradition. He also had a pronounced gift for Romanticism, which flowered in his Piano Concerto no. 3 and *Romeo and Juliet* ballet score.

Prokofiev, who had left Russia after the 1917 revolution, returned in 1933, and he ran into trouble with Soviet authorities over his Modernist tendencies. Despite such patriotic works as the film score to *Alexander Nevsky* (later fashioned into a cantata) and the stirring Symphony no. 5, Prokofiev's last years were spent under a cloud of official disdain. Ironically, he died a few hours before his nemesis, Joseph Stalin.

Sergei Rachmaninoff (1873–1943): He was the last of the Russian Romantics, maintaining his unabashedly lyrical style well into the twentieth century, when that made him an anomaly. He studied piano and composition, winning the admiration of Tchaikovsky and others. Some of his earliest compositions proved enormously successful, especially the brooding Prelude in C-sharp Minor for piano (Rachmaninoff soon grew to despise its popularity). But when his Symphony no. 1 had a disastrous premiere, he went into a severe depression that was conquered only through hypnosis.

He bounced back with the Piano Concerto no. 2, which remains one of the best-loved works in all of classical music. Concerto no. 3 likewise entered the repertoire forcefully (and won renewed appreciation after the 1990s hit film *Shine*). Rachmaninoff's inexhaustible supply of often melancholy melodies yielded such masterpieces of late-Romantic thought as the Symphony no. 2. Toward the end of his life, he revealed a new, more concise and brilliant style in the *Rhapsody on a Theme of Paganini* for piano and orchestra and the *Symphonic Dances* for orchestra.

Rachmaninoff was also one of the twentieth century's greatest pianists. He had a huge sound and a formidable technique (aided by very large hands), as well as an aristocratic way of phrasing. Although he was a sober presence onstage, stern of face, and barely moving his body as he played, the public responded enthusiastically to him. A significant amount of his keyboard artistry is preserved on cherished recordings.

Maurice Ravel (1875–1937): Like fellow Frenchman Debussy, Ravel was greatly impressed by the Javanese sounds he heard at the 1889 Paris World Exposition. He also absorbed lots of Russian influences, especially Rimsky-Korsakov's orchestration. When he added his own distinctive ideas to this mix, he produced music that was striking in its originality and its departure from conventional harmony and structure. This put him at odds with the French musical establishment, which was having enough trouble absorbing Debussy. But Ravel held his course, wearing the label "ultra-Modernist" nonchalantly.

Not really an Impressionist (only a few pieces fit that description neatly), he was an astute colorist and sound-painter, as his String Quartet and dazzling piano piece *Gaspard de la nuit* demonstrate. His *Daphnis et Chloe* set a new standard for ultra-Modern music, with its luscious harmonic ideas and often rapturous effects. When the Jazz Age dawned, Ravel was all ears; his Piano Concerto is wonderfully spiced by jazzy touches.

The composer also had a gift for harking back to distant musical times, such as in *Le Tombeau de Couperin*, an homage to the Baroque French composer Francois Couperin. *Bolero*, an orchestral showpiece that contains one long theme and an unvaried dance rhythm, represented a daring experiment at the time; it provoked heated debate, but wowed the general public. With such works, Ravel, a very short man, left a sizable mark.

Nikolai Rimsky-Korsakov (1844–1908): Like Mussorgsky, Rimsky-Korsakov first embarked on a military career—in his case, the Russian navy—but came in contact with an influential composer. In short order, Rimsky-Korsakov began composing and, at twenty-seven, was appointed professor of composition at the St. Petersburg Conservatory; he was so inexperienced that he had to study secretly all the time to catch up with his students.

The study paid off, and he was soon using an orchestra like a painter to apply color after scintillating color. His *Capriccio espagnol* is a dazzling view of Spain through Russian eyes; *Scheherezade*, an enormous tone poem based on the Arab folk-tale of the *Thousand and One Nights*, provides a textbook model on the art of orchestration (it's also one of the most melodious and entertaining works in the repertoire).

Arnold Schoenberg (1874–1951): The Austrian-born Schoenberg was the most famous, and reviled, revolutionary in all of music, changing the entire course of musical thought in the twentieth century. He was essentially self-taught and revealed individuality almost from the start. One of his first works, *Transfigured Night* for strings, stirred debate due to its diffuse harmonic language, a kind of super-stretched version of the Wagner/Mahler style. A few years later, Schoenberg was provoking near riots with pieces that stretched conventional boundaries much further; *Pierrot Lunaire*, for example, based on surrealist poems, called for a cross between singing and speaking on the part of the soloist.

Gradually, Schoenberg crossed over the outer edges of Western music altogether and created his twelve-tone technique that produced a new, atonal language to replace nearly every vestige of traditional harmony. Music would no longer revolve around a specific key. The mathematical ingenuity of the system and the endless possibilities for expression attracted a number of disciples over the years; for several decades in the middle of the twentieth century, twelve-tone music was virtually the only sanctioned style at leading music conservatories, evidence of Schoenberg's impact.

Most audiences rebelled, however, against his carefully considered atonality, which reached an imposing breadth of inventiveness in such masterworks as *Variations for Orchestra* and the Violin Concerto. But Schoenberg, who settled in the United States after fleeing the Nazis, held out hope that his music would one day be widely popular.

Franz Schubert (1797–1828): Like Mozart, Schubert lived much too short a life: He died of syphilis at thirty-one. But, also like Mozart, he produced several lifetimes' worth of indelible music. Schubert's musical path started as a choirboy in his native Vienna; he wrote his first compositions before he was fifteen. He became greatly interested in writing songs for voice and piano and produced his first masterpieces in the genre by the time he was eighteen.

By making the piano part equally important to the voice and finding telling ways to convey the sense of the words, Schubert elevated the song form to high art. He eventually produced more than six hundred lieder. Among the finest are *Gretchen at the Spinning Wheel, Serenade*, and *The Erl King* (which enables a single singer to delineate four different characters and the piano to evoke the galloping of a horse), as well as two "song cycles"—*Die schone Mullerin* and *Winterreise.*

Schubert also excelled at writing symphonies. The two surviving movements of no. 8, the *Unfinished*, reveal a poetic power that prefigures the Romantic movement; no. 9, called *The Great*, easily ranks alongside the finest of Beethoven's in terms of content, scope, and impact.

Schubert's piano sonatas and chamber works likewise reveal ingenuity of design and effortless melodic invention. Examples include String Quartet no. 14, called *Death and the Maiden* (one of the movements uses the music of a Schubert song with that name); the *Trout* Quintet for piano and strings (again, the title refers to a song that provides melodic material); and the String Quintet.

Robert Schumann (1810–1856): The German composer managed to produce some of the most important works of the Romantic era despite repeated bouts of depression; a freakish hand injury that destroyed any chance for a career as a pianist (he used a contraption to strengthen his hands and only succeeded in dislocating a finger); a protracted, eventually legal, battle over his attempt to marry the daughter of his piano teacher; and a suicide attempt. (In the end, he succumbed to mental illness.)

Schumann's music revealed a passionate streak that found abundant outlet in his four symphonies. His vocal music ascended poetic heights; after Schubert, he was the most gifted lieder composer (*Widmung* and the song cycle *Dichterliebe* illustrate this superbly). His solo-piano music, notably *Carnaval*, is rich in character and technical panache. Although he wasn't able to perform as a pianist (his wife Clara, an exceptional keyboard talent, championed his works), Schumann understood the instrument intuitively and helped widen its scope.

His chamber works are of great quality, notably the Quintet for Piano and Strings; his Piano Concerto is among the noblest in the repertoire. Schumann helped to found an important music journal in Germany and was a perceptive, provocative critic, one of the first to recognize in print the genius of Chopin and Brahms.

Dmitri Shostakovich (1906–1975): In terms of intellectual and musical sophistication, as well as emotional potency, Shostakovich ranks very near the top of classical composers in all of history, not just the twentieth. He excelled at conservatory in piano and composition; his graduation piece, the energetic, eclectic Symphony no. 1, quickly signaled the arrival of a fresh musical force in the Soviet Union. His Piano Concerto no. 1, with its surprising, nearly coequal solo part for trumpet, further enhanced his reputation.

But following the premiere of a brutal and bleak opera, *Lady Macbeth of Mtsensk*, which offended Stalin, Shostakovich was officially rebuked. He made amends, temporarily, with his Symphony no. 5; the ironic subtext of the music went over the heads of the authorities. Periodically throughout the rest of his life, Shostakovich had to worry about Soviet reactions to his work; when he confronted Russian anti-Semitism in his unsettling Symphony no. 13 (*Babi Yar*), government officials took a particularly dim view.

Shostakovich owed a certain debt to Mahler, whose expansive symphonies, with their juxtaposition of tragedy and sardonic humor, beauty, and banality served as a potent model. The Seventh, Eighth, and Tenth symphonies are exceptional examples. The Russian composer's fifteen string quartets are among the most important contributions to that genre since Beethoven; other chamber works, notably the Piano Trio no. 2, Piano Quintet, and Viola Sonata, also reveal his mastery of form and breadth of content

Jean Sibelius (1865–1957): Sibelius captured the granitic beauty of his native Finland in tone poems and symphonies of uncommon power. One of his earliest masterworks, *Finlandia*, served as a rallying cry for Finns who wanted to end the Russian domination of their country; Sibelius's emotion-packed Symphony no. 2 likewise was heard as a patriotic statement. But there was much more to Sibelius than his nationalism. A natural talent who had established himself as a musical force in his twenties, Sibelius revealed a sturdy command of orchestration and a flair for developing musical statements out of small components.

His Violin Concerto quickly entered the repertoire, while his remaining symphonies, especially no. 5, were awaited eagerly by an international audience. Sibelius had the distinction of being one of the most lionized of composers while he was actually alive to enjoy it, but he stopped composing after 1925, living his last three decades away from the limelight.

John Philip Sousa (1854–1932): Military bands were marching to music long before Sousa, but they never had so many great tunes to play until this Washington, D.C., native came along. Sousa offered much more than a flair for melody, though; he earned his nickname "The March King" by taking what had been a routine musical form and giving it an abundance of character, instrumental coloring, and structural cohesiveness. Like "The Waltz King," Johann Strauss, Jr., Sousa transformed a type of music that had previously been utilitarian in nature and made it worthy of the concert hall. Sousa's band toured the world at the turn of the twentieth century, delighting audiences with such irresistible pieces as *Stars and Stripes Forever, The Liberty Bell*, and *The Washington Post March*.

Sousa also wrote several operettas, which have attracted re-

newed interest in recent years, and helped to develop a kind of
tuba still in use by bands everywhere—the sousaphone.

Johann Strauss, Jr. (1825–1899): Like father, like son—only better.
Johann the elder had established himself as the reigning composer of Viennese dance music—waltzes, mostly, along with
polkas and galops—and was not particularly keen on competition from his youngest son. So Johann, Jr., who wrote his first
waltz at the age of six, studied music in secret with the concertmaster of his father's orchestra. After Johann, Sr. deserted
his family, Johann, Jr. was free to pursue a musical career in
the open. He formed an orchestra that rivaled his father's; after
the elder's death, the two ensembles were merged and Johann,
Jr. became the undisputed "Waltz King."

There is much more to a Strauss waltz than good tunes and
a steady beat. There is a clear-cut formal structure—a fairly
slow, sometimes nostalgic, introduction; a series of individual
waltzes (usually five) linked together; then a quick reprise of
parts from all the waltzes and a big finish. Strauss had such an
endless supply of memorable melodies and such a colorful flair
for orchestration that he accumulated an astonishing stream of
hits, true masterpieces of their kind. *Tales from the Vienna
Woods, The Emperor Waltzes*, and *The Blue Danube* are among
the best loved.

Richard Strauss (1864–1949): An early bloomer, Strauss was composing by the time he was six; at sixteen, he heard some of his
works performed in his hometown of Munich. Like Mahler,
Strauss became a conductor and earned a good living from it,
enabling him to compose in his spare time. He scored an instant
success with his tone poem *Don Juan* when he was just twenty-

five, revealing a startling ear for orchestral coloring and a fertile vein of melody; his embrace of Richard Wagner's ideas about harmony and recurring themes caused him to be dubbed "Richard the Second."

Strauss went on to make several other ambitious symphonic poems out of literary works, among them *Don Quixote, Also Sprach Zarathustra*, and *Death and Transfiguration*. He aroused not entirely unwelcome controversy when he dared to make himself the subject of two eventful orchestral pieces—*Ein Heldenleben* ("A Hero's Life") and *Symphonia Domestica* (which put his family life, including some whoopee with his wife, out in the open for all to hear). Strauss went on to devote much of his attention to opera, and throughout his long life he also produced superb songs for voice and piano (or orchestra); the *Four Last Songs*, written just before he died, are particularly sublime. Although tainted by his early association with the Nazi regime, Strauss never lost his reputation as the last of the great Romantic composers.

Igor Stravinsky (1882–1971): If one composer can be named the greatest of the twentieth century, it would have to be Stravinsky. Born in Russia, but most active in Paris and then the United States, Stravinsky led a revolution every bit as radical as Schoenberg's, but one that was far more successful with the public and perhaps far more influential on other composers. He took the essential ingredients of Western musical tradition—harmony, melody, and rhythm—and liberated all of them.

Stravinsky's father, a noted opera singer, wanted his son to study law; Stravinsky obliged for a time, but was drawn to music and eventually studied with Rimsky-Korsakov. A commission from celebrated ballet impresario Sergei Diaghilev led to Stravinsky's first masterwork, *The Firebird.*

That was followed by two more Diaghilev ballets in Paris: *Petroushka*, with its strong taste of irony and bracing harmonies, and, in 1913, *The Rite of Spring*, which had one of the most controversial premieres in music history. The latter turned the music world on its ear thanks to constant shifts in rhythm and fiercely biting chords.

Like Picasso, Stravinsky went through several stylistic periods. The brashness of *Rite of Spring* and other pieces was followed by a neoclassical approach, revisiting musical forms and even the harmonic language of the Baroque era, filtered through twentieth-century ears. The *Pulcinella* ballet and *Dumbarton Oaks* Concerto are prime examples. And in such personal works as *Symphony of Psalms* for chorus and orchestra, the composer revealed yet another side to his musical personality. Later, Stravinsky explored Schoenberg's twelve-tone method in such striking works as *Agon* (another ballet score). There is throughout Stravinsky's output an unending inquisitiveness and assurance of technique. He helped to determine the breadth of "modern music" in the twentieth century.

Peter Ilych Tchaikovsky (1840–1893): The Russian-born Tchaikovsky was a Romantic in every sense, with his heart on his sleeve and, quite regularly, tears in his eyes. Like a few other composers, he was pushed by his family into law studies and held a job for a while with the Ministry of Justice in St. Petersburg. But he also studied music on the side, and eventually devoted all of his attention to it. His earliest works, notably the *Romeo and Juliet* Fantasy-Overture and Piano Concerto no. 1, aroused attention for their explosive passion. Many of his works took a long time to win over the public and the press, but, once in the repertoire, nothing could dislodge them.

With his Violin Concerto and Fourth, Fifth, and Sixth symphonies, Tchaikovsky reached heights of intensity; his ballet scores, *Sleeping Beauty*, *Swan Lake*, and *The Nutcracker*, likewise overflow with melody and prismatic orchestration. He was not a musical trailblazer except, perhaps, in his Sixth Symphony, which broke away substantially from conventional expectations. And some of his compositions went a bit over the top in search of crowd-pleasing effects (the *1812* Overture comes quickly to mind).

But there is a basic honesty and openness about virtually all of Tchaikovsky's music. He was not always honest with himself, however; in attempting to conceal his homosexuality, he agreed to marry a fawning, unstable admirer, who drove him to a suicide attempt after two months. There was another woman in Tchaikovsky's life, though—a wealthy patroness who provided much-needed financial and emotional support (by correspondence) for several years, before suddenly breaking it off.

Tchaikovsky's death, apparently from cholera, has fueled much debate; theories of suicide, accidental or coerced, have abounded. Whatever the circumstances, he died at the peak of his artistic powers.

Ralph Vaughan Williams (1872–1958): Along with Elgar and Britten, Vaughan Williams was one of England's most gifted composers. Following his academic studies, he spent a long time collecting English songs—hundreds of them. He used them in his own music both directly (the luscious *Fantasia on "Greensleeves"*) or only by suggestion, making much of his work subtly nationalistic in character.

At his most Romantic, Vaughan Williams was responsible for such twentieth-century classics as the *Fantasia on a Theme of Thomas Tallis* for strings and *The Lark Ascending* for violin and orchestra. His nine symphonies contain many distinctive ideas; the reflective Fifth, written in the midst of World War II, makes a particularly haunting impression. Neither starkly Modern nor unwaveringly Romantic, the music of Vaughan Williams uniquely combined echoes of the past with the techniques and sensibilities of his own time.

Antonio Vivaldi (1678–1741): One of the most prolific composers of the Baroque era, Vivaldi started out in a clerical career—after being ordained in 1703, he was nicknamed "The Red Priest," on account of his hair. He didn't stay active in the priesthood for long, however. An old, probably apocryphal, story says that while saying Mass one day in his native Venice, he suddenly walked off the altar to jot down a melody that had popped into his head. No question, his heart was not in clerical duties.

He spent most of his life composing and produced an enormous amount of music, including about five hundred concertos. (The joke goes he really just wrote one concerto five hundred times, but careful listening refutes that easily enough.) He made a lasting mark with his delectably descriptive set of violin concertos called *The Four Seasons*.

Other gems are the sparkling *Gloria* for chorus and orchestra, originally written for a girls' orphanage in Venice, where he served as music director; and the Guitar Concerto in D Major (the slow movement alone reveals Vivaldi's admirable gift for elegant melody).

Richard Wagner (1813–1883): Although the German-born composer was immortalized by his epic operas, he left his mark on all varieties of classical music. Without him, there would have been no Bruckner, Mahler, Richard Strauss, or many others. Wagner vastly enhanced the harmonic language of music, clearing paths to new ways of molding chords and of extending melody. A master of orchestration, the purely instrumental music from his operas is as meaningful and substantive as many other composers' symphonies.

The aural universe he chartered with the Prelude to *Tristan und Isolde* essentially changed the course of music history, pushing Romanticism into a new, more intense realm and effectively pointing toward the twentieth century—all the more remarkable when you consider it was first heard in 1865. And his development of the *leitmotif* in opera to provide characters or ideas with individual themes in his operas was picked up by other composers for use in nonoperatic ways. The Prelude to *Die Meistersinger*, with its spirited interweaving of multiple themes, likewise influenced many who came after him.

Ellen Taaffe Zwilich (b. 1939): The Florida-born Zwilich, who started her career as a violinist, achieved significant firsts—the first woman to receive a doctorate in composition from New York's famed Juilliard School of Music; the first woman to receive the Pulitzer Prize in music (for her Symphony no. 1 of 1982).

Her music moved gradually from a complex, atonal style to a more accessible one characterized by tightly organized development of themes and expressive gestures. Her concise and arresting Symphony no. 3, written for the New York Philharmonic's 150th anniversary, and Trio for Violin, Cello, and Piano exemplify her craft. *A Peanuts Gallery*, based on characters in the Charles Schulz comic strip, reveals the composer's lighter, witty side.

SIX

The Performers

If a tree falls in a forest and no one hears it, some folks like to argue, it doesn't make a sound. Likewise, if a composition is not performed, it really doesn't exist. Music needs to be given life by singers, instrumentalists, chamber ensembles, orchestras, and conductors. The history of music is very much the history of musicians.

The following list, once again unavoidably subjective, offers a glimpse into this legion of classical performers. The majority of those mentioned can be heard on recordings, allowing us to experience their talent directly. But you'll also read about several people who preceded the dawn of recorded sound; their achievements were clearly as indelible as those preserved on disc, and these bygone figures played a substantial role in developing lasting tastes and standards in musical performance. Some of the artists here were composers, too, but are included because their greatest fame came from their performing careers.

Obviously, group music making is a major part of the performance scene—from the world's oldest ensemble, the Dresden Staatskapelle (founded 1548) to the Vienna and New York philharmonics (both started in 1842); from the emergence of professional string quartets in the nineteenth century to the many first-rate chamber music ensembles of today. But, to avoid overload, this list is limited to individuals.

Remember, these fifty men and women represent just a small sample of classical talents, past and present. There's plenty more where these came from.

Maurice Andre (b. 1933): Music for trumpet rarely took centerstage before this Frenchman burst on the scene in the 1950s with his gleaming tone and impeccable technique. He recorded dozens of trumpet concertos, many of them long neglected, and made a particularly memorable impression in the Baroque repertoire.

Martha Argerich (b. 1941): The Argentinean-born pianist enjoys something of a cult status due to the incredible virtuosity and intensity of her playing, as well as the rarity of her public performances (the joke is that Argerich is available for a limited number of cancellations each season). Since winning the Chopin Competition in Warsaw in 1965, she has been greatly admired for her interpretations of the Romantic repertoire, many preserved on disc. In recent years, she has avoided solo recitals but collaborates on occasion with orchestras and in chamber music.

Vladimir Ashkenazy (b. 1937): The Russian-born pianist rose to prominence after sharing first prize at the Tchaikovsky Competition in Moscow in 1962. His combination of technical elan and keenly poetic instincts made him especially valued in the works of Chopin, which he recorded extensively. Since the 1980s, Ashkenazy has concentrated more on conducting than piano performance, enjoying a second successful career.

Thomas Beecham (1879–1961): One of the most engaging podium talents of the twentieth century, Beecham was largely self-taught and initially made his name by leading orchestras he founded with his own money, including the London Philharmonic and Royal Philharmonic. The British conductor earned especially high marks for his sunny interpretations of Mozart and Haydn, as well as for championing the subtly colored music of Frederick Delius. Beecham also had an unusual knack for treating "light" music with the same care and respect he accorded the rest of the orchestral repertoire. He was equally celebrated for a quick, sometimes ruthless wit. Sample: "You have between your legs the most sensitive instrument known to man," he said to a cowering cellist, "and all you can do is sit there and scratch it."

Joshua Bell (b. 1967): Born in Bloomington, Indiana, where he went on to study violin at Indiana University with Josef Gingold, one of the most respected pedagogues in the business, Bell was on the way to an impressive career by the time he entered his teens. There was from the start something unusually lyrical about Bell's playing, a sweetness and warmth, in addition to refined technical facility, that earned him a large following. In addition to performing and recording the standard violin repertoire, he gave the world premiere of the Violin Concerto by important British composer Nicholas Maw in 1993 and was the soloist in John Corigliano's Academy Award–winning film score for *The Red Violin* in 1998.

Leonard Bernstein (1918–1990): Astonishingly gifted as a conductor, composer, pianist, and teacher, Bernstein was an irreplaceable force in the music world. His personal charisma and widely publicized espousal of liberal political causes helped make him one of the most famous classical musicians in the twentieth century. He became front-page news when he stepped in to conduct the New York Philharmonic for an ailing Bruno Walter in 1943; he went on to become the first American music director of that orchestra (1958–69).

Among his hundreds of vitality-packed recordings was the first complete cycle of Mahler symphonies, which helped significantly to spark greater (and still ongoing) popularity for that composer. Bernstein's witty, inventive, and highly informative series of nationally televised *Young People's Concerts* with the New York Philharmonic introduced more than one generation to classical music. Bernstein cultivated a remarkable rapport with the Vienna Philharmonic as well, also liberally documented on recordings. Known for his wild leaps on the podium (nicknamed "The Lenny Dance"), Bernstein's concerts were always events. Although his preference for slow tempos and sometimes extremely emotional phrasing in his later years did not suit all tastes, the results could be profound.

Bernstein was also one of the most popular American composers. He had a particular flair for the Broadway idiom; his scores to *On the Town, Candide*, and, especially, *West Side Story*, contained indelible melodies and a vibrant, rhythmic spark. Bernstein's determined efforts as a symphonic writer produced uneven, but almost always engaging, works; his *Mass*, a "theater piece" for eclectic vocal and instrumental forces, reflects the composer's continual striving for answers to questions of life, faith, and peace.

Hans von Bulow (1830–1894): This great German pianist and conductor had perhaps the longest running rendezvous with musical destiny of anyone. As a conductor, Bulow led the first performances of Wagner's operas *Tristan und Isolde* and *Die Meistersinger*, and didn't even seem terribly upset that his wife, the illegitimate daughter of Franz Liszt, was sleeping with Wagner at the time. Bulow also championed the works of Brahms from the podium.

As a pianist, he made history by premiering Tchaikovsky's Piano Concerto no. 1 in Boston in 1875, helping to establish the concerto in the repertoire. He didn't make life easy for the musicians he conducted; his orchestra at Meiningen in Germany had to play from memory—standing up. And Bulow wasn't all that friendly to his listeners; he was known to castigate audiences if he thought they were misbehaving, a practice that would keep him very busy in concert halls today.

Pablo Casals (1876–1973): The Spanish-born virtuoso was history's first cello superstar. By 1899, his reputation for flawless technique and uncommonly communicative phrasing was firmly established. He became particularly noted for popularizing the unaccompanied cello suites of Bach, works previously appreciated primarily by connoisseurs.

The depth of feeling in his cello-playing was matched by an intense commitment to peace in the world. An outspoken opponent of fascism, which drove him from his native country, Casals was one of the most loved and admired musicians of the twentieth century.

Van Cliburn (b. 1934): It may seem like ancient history now, but the Cold War during the 1950s was an exceedingly real, often tense time. The competition between the Soviet Union and United States took an unexpected turn when a tall, boyish, charming, Texan pianist became the first American to win the 1958 Tchaikovsky Competition in Moscow, demonstrating a thunderous tone and sweeping, romantic style.

Cliburn returned home a national hero, treated to a ticker-tape parade down Broadway, and embarked on a busy round of concertizing and recording. Although the pianist's enormous potential was never fully realized (his career was essentially over by the 1970s), he clearly left his mark on music. In 1962, he founded one of the world's leading events for budding pianists, the Van Cliburn Competition in Texas.

Jacqueline Du Pre (1945–1987): This British cellist enjoyed a short but sensational career, winning intense appreciation from audiences for her large tone, sterling technique, and unabashedly emotional playing style. Her interpretation of Elgar's Cello Concerto was especially acclaimed. In 1972, after little more than a decade of performing, Du Pre was forced to retire after being diagnosed with multiple sclerosis. Her complicated and painful private life became the subject of a controversial film in 1998, *Hilary and Jackie.*

Dietrich Fischer-Dieskau (b. 1925): This German baritone came to represent the epitome of a lieder singer in the twentieth century. His repertoire of well over one thousand art songs, primarily of the German repertoire, was amply preserved on recordings (including nearly all of Schubert's lieder). His recitals were known to sell out in a matter of hours and became an almost spiritual experience for listeners.

With his resonant voice and attentiveness to the many nuances of words and melodies, Fischer-Dieskau communicated the innermost beauty of lieder as few vocal artists could. He also excelled in opera, and Benjamin Britten wrote the baritone part in the *War Requiem* of 1962 expressly for him. After retiring from singing, Fischer-Dieskau concentrated on teaching and occasional conducting.

Wilhelm Furtwängler (1886–1954): One of the most inspired and inspiring, not to mention controversial, conductors of the twentieth century, Furtwängler represented an intensely personal style of interpreting music that has gone largely out of fashion today. That style, with its roots in nineteenth-century Romanticism, yielded performances quite unlike anyone else's. Furtwängler's Beethoven and Brahms were epic dramas on a scale with Wagner operas, which he also conducted with hypnotic intensity and breadth of feeling.

But his decision to remain in Nazi Germany as conductor of the famed Berlin Philharmonic cost him dearly in international stature. Despite being cleared by a de-Nazification tribunal after the war, Furtwängler faced considerable hostility in some corners. Not even Jewish violinist Yehudi Menuhin's spirited defense of him could entirely overcome the stigma. His recordings, however, have come to be highly prized by collectors, valued for their individuality, expressive heat, and uplifting spirituality.

James Galway (b. 1939): The second superstar flutist, after Rampal, this Irishman played for six years in the Berlin Philharmonic before launching an extraordinarily successful solo career in 1975. His technical facility, warm phrasing, and irresistible, impish charm combined to make him a favorite with audiences and a bestselling recording artist. Several composers wrote works for him; among them is John Corigliano's *Pied Piper Fantasy*.

John Eliot Gardiner (b. 1943): The British conductor has long been at the forefront of the historical authenticity movement—the effort to re-create not just the sounds, but the style, of music making from the seventeenth, eighteenth, and nineteenth centuries. (Two other British conductors, Christopher Hogwood and Roger Norrington, have also earned distinction in this field.) Gardiner's combination of scholarship and musical vitality have made his performances of Bach and Beethoven particularly effective and revelatory.

Louis Moreau Gottschalk (1829–1869): Perhaps the first American musician to impress Europeans, the New Orleans–born pianist won favorable comparisons with Chopin when he debuted in Paris at the age of fifteen. Gottschalk wasn't allowed into the Paris Conservatoire to study, because of anti-American bias, but that didn't slow down his career. His triumphant concerts featured lots of his own piano compositions, which captured the flavor of American folk music and, especially, Latin American influences.

He returned to his native country in the early 1850s and became its first keyboard star; at the peak of his fame, he traveled nearly one hundred thousand miles by train to give more than one thousand performances—in only three years. Accused of improper conduct with a young lady in 1865, Gottschalk hightailed it for South America, where he died.

Glenn Gould (1932–1982): The Canadian pianist was, in just about every sense, a genius. He challenged conventionality in music by means of an intensely inquisitive mind and a downright quirky personality. Even the way he sat at the piano was unusual, very low and hunched over. He had a habit of singing along noisily as he played. But nothing really distracted from the seriousness and inventiveness of his playing.

Gould became famed for his Bach performances, finding a particularly startling level of virtuosity and beauty of phrasing in the *Goldberg* Variations. In 1964, he abandoned live performance in favor of painstaking work in the recording studio. His withdrawal from the public spotlight fueled his cult status, which continues to this day.

Jascha Heifetz (1901–1987): Even folks who wouldn't be caught dead at a violin recital know the name Heifetz. It is synonymous with technical prowess, flawless intonation, penetrating tone, and thoughtful interpretation. The Russian-born, naturalized-American fiddler started as a child prodigy and developed into a commanding artist with a patrician aura.

His poker-faced manner onstage and his preference for a literal, rather than deeply personal, approach to a score did not impress everyone equally, but the effortless virtuosity and keen intelligence of a Heifetz performance set standards against which all violinists are measured. His chamber-music activity was also treasured; he appeared frequently with celebrated cellists Emanuel Feuermann and Gregor Piatigorsky and pianist Arthur Rubinstein. Heifetz's many recordings provide a lasting testament to his achievements.

Josef Hofmann (1876–1957): At the age of eleven, this Polish-born pianist made his American debut with a concert at the Metropolitan Opera House and became an overnight sensation. He proceeded to play so many concerts that the Society for the Prevention of Cruelty to Children intervened. He reemerged as a soloist when he was eighteen and became a fixture on the concert circuit, praised for his faithfulness to the printed score (something of a novelty at the turn of the twentieth century) and his ability to summon the most delicate or most explosive sounds possible from the keyboard. He later became director of the Curtis Institute of Music in Philadelphia, one of the more fertile conservatories in the country.

Vladimir Horowitz (1903–1989): This spectacularly gifted Russian-born, naturalized-American pianist represented for many the epitome of keyboard virtuosity. He could summon a thunderous, yet well-controlled sound from the keyboard and fly through complicated passages with breathtaking ease. His fame seemed to grow even larger during periodic retirements, for a variety of personal reasons, from the concert stage; the longest absence, twelve years, ended with a sensational, now legendary reemergence at Carnegie Hall in 1965.

In 1986, he returned to his native Russia, where he played a recital telecast worldwide. In the super-Romantic repertoire of Liszt and Rachmaninoff, Horowitz was without equal; in addition to spectacular pianistic fireworks, he could also produce positively delicate, poetic sounds, as in his endearing account of Schumann's *Traumerei*, which he often played as an encore. An extensive discography preserves the Horowitz magic.

Joseph Joachim (1831–1907): One of the most historically significant violinists, the Hungarian-born Joachim was more than a virtuoso, he was an inspiration. He established Beethoven's Violin Concerto firmly in the repertoire (the work had not been widely appreciated before); he premiered the Violin Concerto by Brahms, who wrote much of his violin music with Joachim's playing in mind.

His technical poise and, above all, ability to phrase a melodic line with the finesse and warmth of a great singer endeared him to public and critics alike. The violinist also had a significant impact on chamber music as leader of the Joachim Quartet, which was renowned for its cohesiveness and incisiveness.

Herbert von Karajan (1908–1989): The most-recorded conductor in history, the Austrian-born Karajan began his career just about the time Hitler was rising to power and joined the Nazi Party to further his advancement. Karajan successfully overcame any stigmas after the war and, following Wilhelm Furtwängler's death, took over the Berlin Philharmonic in 1954. As "conductor for life," he polished it into the world's most technically proficient orchestra. Karajan's interpretations could become too obsessed with perfection but, at his best, he achieved a combination of brilliance and depth.

Evgeny Kissin (b. 1971): Recordings made when the Russian-born pianist was a child prodigy began circulating in the early 1980s, signaling the arrival of an unusually promising artist who already had musically mature ideas and a super-virtuoso technique. Kissin's spectacular Carnegie Hall debut in 1990 confirmed that he was a major new star. His performances and recordings continue to earn widespread praise.

Fritz Kreisler (1875–1962): The Austrian violinist became a household name thanks to the invention of the gramophone; his recordings were among the most popular released in the days of Victrolas and easily breakable 78 rpm records.

In addition to offering eloquent interpretations of Beethoven, Elgar (who wrote his Violin Concerto for him), and many others, Kreisler had a knack for composing short, charming, evocative, violin pieces, which were featured in his recitals and still attract violinists. (Kreisler pretended that some of these pieces were written by eighteenth-century composers, and fooled quite a few people before coming clean.) The stylish cadenzas he wrote for the Beethoven and Brahms concertos continue to be favored by many fiddlers to this day.

Wanda Landowska (1879–1959): She started out as a pianist, but by 1912 had developed a fascination with the harpsichord, an instrument then largely confined to museums. The Polish-born virtuoso almost singlehandedly revived interest in the harpsichord and the music written for it, especially by Bach. In addition, she commissioned new works from some of the leading composers of her day.

Her recitals took on the air of religious services as she communed with Bach, instead of merely playing the notes. Landowska established a center for the study of early music and became a much sought-after teacher. Although later scholarship would question her approach to Baroque music (she took many personal liberties with a score), the vibrant nature and technical elan of her playing—preserved on recordings—remain intensely appealing.

Yo-Yo Ma (b. 1955): Born in Paris of Chinese parents, this richly talented cellist gave his first recital at six and made his New York Philharmonic debut at twelve, with Bernstein conducting. His emotive playing style and effortless technical command have endeared him to audiences ever since. Ma is equally at home in solo, concerto, and chamber repertoire from all time periods. His inquisitiveness has taken him in many unusual directions, including jazz, folk, and World music.

Yehudi Menuhin (1916–1999): A child prodigy whose precocious abilities had critics scrambling for superlatives, the American-born violinist made the transition to mature artist smoothly, maintaining his technical aplomb and innate sense of interpretive eloquence. His recordings of Elgar's Violin Concerto (while still a teenager, with the composer conducting) and Beethoven's Violin Concerto (with Wilhelm Furtwängler conducting) have enjoyed widespread admiration for their insight.

His experimentation with Indian music, collaborating with sitar virtuoso Ravi Shankar, was typical of the violinist's breadth. And, like Pablo Casals, Menuhin became as revered for his humanitarian concerns as for his musicianship.

Dimitri Mitropoulos (1896–1960): This Greek-American conductor was one of the most interesting personalities to be found on a podium from the 1930s until his sad death of a heart attack while rehearsing Gustav Mahler's Symphony no. 3 in Milan. Mitropoulos was one of the few conductors to champion Mahler's music before it became widely popular; his interpretations of that composer and many others were notable for their emotional force and individualistic phrasing. Mitropoulos served with distinction as music director of the Minneapolis Symphony and, later, the New York Philharmonic.

David Oistrakh (1908–1974): Often ranked alongside Heifetz in terms of flawless technique and abundant musicality, the Russian-born violinist came to attention in 1937 after winning an international competition in Belgium. Back in the Soviet Union, he won the public's admiration and affection by playing concerts in Leningrad during the dark days under siege of German forces during World War II. Several leading composers wrote works for Oistrakh, including Shostakovich and Prokofiev.

Ignaz Paderewski (1860–1941): This Polish piano virtuoso had roughly the same effect on women that Ricky Martin had at the turn of the twenty-first century; Paderewski was nearly done in by a mob of adoring ladies after a Carnegie Hall recital in 1902. With a marvelous shock of reddish blond hair adding drama to his appearance, Paderewski was a publicist's dream. His earnings were, for their time, astronomical.

He made many recordings, which do not necessarily explain what all the fuss was about. He did not have a flawless technique, and he took extensive liberties with music—changing rhythms freely, for example—that bothered some listeners in his day, and some listeners since. But there was nonetheless an aristocratic quality to his pianism that still comes through effectively on those old records. Paderewski enjoyed a second career in government, serving for a time as premier of the newly independent state of Poland after World War I and president of its parliament-in-exile during the first year of World War II.

Niccolo Paganini (1782–1840): Just as Liszt expanded the expressive and technical horizons of the piano, Paganini changed forever the very nature of violin playing; every fiddler who came after him was, in one way or another, influenced by what Paganini composed for the instrument and how he played it. The public simply worshipped him.

His facility was so astonishing, seemingly superhuman, that some folks honestly believed he had sold his soul to the devil in exchange for superior virtuosity. (It didn't help that Paganini looked rather vampirelike—a tall, very slender physique, long, black hair, and, following a jawbone operation, a sunken face.) He introduced an unprecedented level of showmanship into the classical music world, but he was also a solid musician, capable of remarkably tender expressiveness.

Murray Perahia (b. 1947): Since the 1970s, this native New Yorker has won intense admiration for his unusually refined piano artistry. Early on, Perahia revealed an intuitive appreciation for the subtlest elements of form and content in the works of Mozart; his recordings of that composer's piano concertos as soloist and conductor of the English Chamber Orchestra enjoy honored status. Although not a super virtuoso in the mold of Horowitz (one of his mentors), Perahia has a disarming command of the keyboard that allows him to focus squarely on musical values. In addition to Mozart, his playing of Bach, Chopin, and Mendelssohn is particularly impressive.

Itzhak Perlman (b. 1945): The Israeli-born violinist overcame a severe handicap (he lost the use of his legs from polio when he was four) to enjoy one of the most successful music careers of the last forty years. He became particularly admired for his golden tone; thoughtful, openhearted interpretations of the Romantic repertoire; and a nonchalant control of even the most fiendishly difficult violin showpieces. Perlman developed a large, devoted following with the public, which takes delight not only in his fiddling, but the humor that is likely to surface, especially in recitals.

Jean-Pierre Rampal (1922–2000): The first superstar flutist, the French-born Rampal became widely celebrated for the purity of his tone and the elegance of his phrasing, especially in the music of Bach and other Baroque composers. Rampal also won many nonclassical fans with his recordings of crossover pieces by jazz man Claude Bolling.

Sviatoslav Richter (1915–1997): The Russian-born Richter, one of the twentieth century's most compelling pianists, was initially interested in painting, which remained a lifelong avocation. He was basically a self-taught pianist until beginning formal studies at the unusually advanced age of twenty-one. He had a sterling, effortless technique and a penetrating musical mind, which made him an authoritative performer of Beethoven, Schubert, Liszt, and Prokofiev. An enigmatic man, he disliked making studio recordings and often gave recitals in small towns with hardly any fanfare.

Mstislav Rostropovich (b. 1927): In addition to being one of the greatest cellists of the twentieth century, this Russian-born musician earned international respect for his ardent support of dissidents in the former Soviet Union, which stripped him and his wife, noted soprano Galina Vishnevskaya, of their Soviet citizenship.

Rostropovich's unusually large, penetrating tone and heartfelt phrasing have made him a favorite interpreter of works by Haydn, Dvořák, and Tchaikovsky. Many twentieth-century composers wrote works for him, including Prokofiev, Shostakovich, and Britten. Rostropovich has also enjoyed a career as a conductor; he was music director of the National Symphony

Orchestra in Washington, D.C., for seventeen years and has guest-conducted most of the world's leading ensembles.

Anton Rubinstein (1829–1894): This Russian pianist is said to be the first to make a fortune from concert fees; he toured Europe and America extensively. Significantly, Rubinstein was famous for making mistakes in performance; he was clearly not obsessed with technical perfection. What made him a star was the poetic weight in his playing, the stunning tone he could get out of an instrument, and the sense of spontaneous musical combustion. Rubinstein also greatly influenced the next generation of Russian musicians.

Arthur Rubinstein (1887–1982): For much of the nineteenth century, the name Rubinstein meant superlative piano playing; it did in the twentieth, too. The earlier Rubinstein (no relation) was Russian, the latter Polish. This Rubinstein, who eventually became an American citizen, was one of the most famous musicians—and personalities—in history. He also was one of the most loved.

To many listeners, Rubinstein was *the* Chopin interpreter. He recorded nearly all of Chopin's works, many of them more than once; his approach to this music was supremely elegant, unfussy, never exaggerated, and virtuosic without being showy. In addition to his extensive recorded legacy, including Spanish and French repertoire, the pianist left two volumes of disarming autobiography.

Pablo de Sarasate (1844–1908): One of the most admired violinists of his time, the Spanish-born Sarasate demonstrated consummate technical elan and a tone of uncommon sweetness. No wonder several leading composers wrote concertos especially for him, including Saint-Saens, Eduard Lalo (the colorful *Symphonie espagnole*), and Max Bruch (the soaring *Scottish Fantasy*). Sarasate also composed one of the most deliciously schmaltzy pieces in the violin repertoire, *Zigeunerweisen* ("Gypsy Airs").

Artur Schnabel (1882–1951): This Austrian-born pianist, who eventually became an American citizen, was, for many people and for a long time, synonymous with the name Beethoven. In the 1930s, he became the first to record the complete Beethoven piano sonatas, recordings that remain benchmarks of stylistic authority. Although not a technically perfect pianist, Schnabel's insight and communicative skill made him one of the most revered musicians of his time. His performances of Mozart and Schubert were as prized as those of Beethoven.

Clara Schumann (1819–1896): Wife of eminent German composer Robert Schumann, Clara was one of the first women to enjoy a successful career as a pianist, at a time when music was very much a man's world. She began as a child prodigy and matured into a notable artist. Clara gave the premiere of her husband's Piano Concerto and, after his death in 1856, championed his music in concerts. She was also renowned for her interpretations of music by Chopin and Brahms (she and Brahms maintained a lifelong, possibly intimate, friendship).

Andres Segovia (1893–1987): The acoustic guitar—like its predecessor, the lute—has had a connection to classical music for centuries (Vivaldi and Paganini were among the noted composers who wrote for the instrument). But it was Segovia who brought it from the sidelines into the spotlight.

The Spanish virtuoso revealed the guitar's innate sensuousness, while demonstrating a technique that made him as impressive as the leading piano or violin stars. In addition to transcribing a lot of music (especially by Bach) originally written for other instruments, Segovia inspired many composers to create works for him, adding immeasurably to the guitar repertoire.

Robert Shaw (1916–1999): The name of this Californian conductor is synonymous with great choral singing. Although Shaw enjoyed abundant success as an orchestral conductor—he served as associate conductor of the Cleveland Orchestra and music director of the Atlanta Symphony Orchestra during his long, distinguished career—he was best known for his work with choruses. The Robert Shaw Chorale, which he founded in 1948 and directed for twenty seasons, set the standard for technical excellence and expressive potency. Shaw worked the same magic with any choral group he directed. Many recordings attest to his rare talent.

Leonard Slatkin (b. 1944): Like Michael Tilson Thomas, who was born the same year and in the same city (Los Angeles), Slatkin has become one of America's best and brightest conductors. For seventeen years, he was music director of the St. Louis Symphony Orchestra, helping to turn a regional ensemble into one of international stature. Slatkin's openness to contemporary composers was a significant part of that tenure, as it has been since he moved on in 1996 to become music director of the National Symphony Orchestra of Washington, D.C. In addition to that position, the articulate, inquisitive Slatkin was named music director of the BBC Symphony Orchestra in 1999.

Georg Solti (1912–1997): Another exceptionally well-recorded conductor, the Hungarian-born Solti achieved his highest fame as longtime music director of the Chicago Symphony Orchestra, 1969–1991. His dynamic leadership proved a superb match for that already distinguished ensemble and helped bring the Chicagoans even greater admiration. Equally compelling as an opera conductor, Solti generated performances of symphonic music notable for their technical precision and burnished sound, with particular emphasis on the brass.

Isaac Stern (1920–2001): Born in Ukraine, Stern came to the United States in his first year. He was studying violin at eight and made his orchestral debut at eleven. By seventeen, he had made his New York recital debut and launched one of the most distinguished careers in American music, admired for his warm violin tone and wide-ranging musical tastes (he premiered numerous twentieth-century works). His hands appeared in the classic 1946 Joan Crawford film *Humoresque*, doing all the violin playing for John Garfield. In the 1960s, Stern was instrumental in saving Carnegie Hall from the wrecking ball and in creating the National Endowment for the Arts.

Leopold Stokowski (1882–1977): One of the most famous conductors of the twentieth century, thanks in no small measure to an appearance on the silver screen with Mickey Mouse, Stokowski combined showmanship and an inquisitive musical mind. British-born and later an American citizen, the conductor led the Philadelphia Orchestra for two decades and developed the trademark lushness of its string tone—forever known as the "Philadelphia Sound."

He conducted the first U.S. performances of such daunting challenges as Mahler's Symphony no. 8 and Schoenberg's *Gurrelieder*, and intrepidly introduced decidedly Modern sounds to a decidedly conservative public. Stokowski's own richly Romantic, prismatic orchestral arrangements of music by Bach raised eyebrows at the time, but remain irresistible to many.

He was the first conductor to be treated very much like a movie star, even before he participated in Walt Disney's animated classic *Fantasia* in 1940 (he was famously linked romantically to Greta Garbo for a time). His long career also included the music directorship of the Houston Symphony and the founding of the American Symphony Orchestra (with that ensemble, he led the first performance of Charles Ives's enormously complex Symphony no. 4—at the age of eighty-three).

George Szell (1897–1970): The Hungarian-born conductor achieved lasting fame as music director of the Cleveland Orchestra from 1946 until his death. On the podium, he was both authoritative and authoritarian; he drove his ensemble very hard, propelling it to the top echelon of orchestras, not just in the United States, but in the world. The strict discipline was complemented by a keen, musical mind and total immersion into the smallest details of a score. Szell's insights into the core Austrian and German repertoire have always been particularly cherished. Numerous recordings attest to the dynamic results the conductor achieved with the Clevelanders during his long tenure.

Yuri Temirkanov (b. 1938): Since his 1968 victory in a conducting competition in his native Russia (then the Soviet Union), Temirkanov has enjoyed a reputation for a galvanizing approach to music that stresses emotional intensity and technical polish. He served as conductor of the Leningrad Symphony Orchestra, the Kirov Opera and Ballet, and then the Leningrad Philharmonic (now called the St. Petersburg Philharmonic). In addition to working with Russian organizations, he has served as principal guest conductor of the Royal Philharmonic in London and became music director of the Baltimore Symphony Orchestra in 2000.

Michael Tilson Thomas (b. 1944): One of the most prodigiously gifted American musicians since Bernstein, Tilson Thomas became the Boston Symphony Orchestra's youngest assistant conductor (at twenty-four) and went on to lead the Buffalo Philharmonic, London Symphony Orchestra, and, starting in 1995, the San Francisco Symphony Orchestra. He also founded the New World Symphony in Miami Beach, "America's Orchestral Academy," an intensive training ensemble for under-thirty, postgraduate musicians; many of them have gone on to become members of orchestras throughout the world.

Tilson Thomas, a strong advocate of new music, has made waves with an "American Mavericks" festival in San Francisco that has included such innovations as collaborations between his orchestra and members of the legendary rock band the Grateful Dead.

Arturo Toscanini (1867–1957): The Italian-born Toscanini, the first universally recognized conductor of the twentieth century, was treated with a rare kind of reverence that wouldn't come close to being matched until the mature years of Leonard Bernstein. Toscanini started out as a cellist but, during a legendary performance of Verdi's *Aida* in Brazil in 1886, took over the baton from a conductor who apparently walked off the job shortly after the opera started. Toscanini finished the performance, conducting from memory. His career was on its way. In addition to heralded work in opera houses, Toscanini enjoyed a fruitful tenure at the helm of the New York Philharmonic and then as conductor of the NBC Symphony Orchestra, specifically created for him and made renowned by regular radio broadcasts.

Toscanini was a megawatt force on the podium; the electricity and tautness of his music making became legendary. He espoused devotion to the printed score, and his avoidance of exaggerations in phrasing represented a dramatic contrast to several of his contemporaries and served as a model for many conductors who came after him. The notorious Toscanini temper and ego did nothing to dampen the respect accorded him by musicians. The conductor's recordings, still readily available, contain dated sound, but timeless lessons in the art of vivid music making.

SEVEN

The Music

There's no such thing as a short list of the greatest classical music. Each era has produced an enormous quantity of scores that can unhesitatingly be called masterpieces. That's one reason classical music is really a lifelong study—and a lifelong reward.

Still, it's possible to zero in on works that, for a variety of reasons, occupy the highest plateau of classical music. Like the most revered examples of architecture or painting over the centuries, such works have never lost their potency: their ability to engage, enlighten, and enrich.

Here's a very selective, subjective list of fifty-five towering compositions, arranged alphabetically by title (the date given with each work reflects the year it was composed, not necessarily first performed or published). If some of the terms mentioned in the entries don't quite register, please refer to the

Classical Music Deconstructed and The Language of Classical Music chapters for clarification.

The creative efforts represented in this list help to define the very essence of classical music and will amply repay the curiosity of any listener.

Appalachian Spring, Aaron Copland (1944): Leaving behind his dissonant style of the early 1920s, Copland developed a simpler, more melodic style, rooted in folk music that was regarded as quintessentially American. A prime demonstration is this score he wrote for a ballet by Martha Graham called *Appalachian Spring*, which has become particularly cherished for its charm, honest sentiments, and enveloping warmth.

The plot of the ballet involves pioneer newlyweds on a farm in Pennsylvania, contemplating life together, being visited by neighbors and a traveling preacher, finally settling down alone in their home, content and ready to face whatever comes. Although the complete, original score for thirteen instruments has much to recommend it, especially in terms of transparent textures, the suite for full orchestra that Copland subsequently fashioned is more commonly heard. The suite, which includes all the main musical highlights of the ballet, including the famous introduction of the old Shaker hymn *Simple Gifts*, finds Copland at his most heartfelt and ingratiating.

Carnaval, op. 9, Robert Schumann (1835): Schumann, who helped to unleash the piano's expressive and coloristic potential, used the keyboard as a kind of psychiatrist's couch, confiding into the instrument his innermost thoughts. Destined for an insane asylum, where he died, Schumann supposedly had a split personality, which he himself characterized as the outgoing "Florestan" and the introspective "Eusebius." Those two characters were reflected in many of Schumann's compositions, nowhere more vividly than in *Carnaval*.

The work consists of nearly two dozen short pieces, all tied together by four notes. Those notes, in German musical notation, spell out ASCH; Ernestine von Fricken, Schumann's girlfriend at the time, came from the town of Asch in Germany. The mileage Schumann gets out of those four notes is quite amazing. Each piece in *Carnaval* has a title. There's one for Ernestine ("Estrella"), and another for Clara Weick ("Clarina"), a teenager who would eventually become Schumann's wife; there's one for Florestan, another for Eusebius; one piece captures Schumann's admiration for Chopin, another for violin virtuoso Paganini. The novel structure and sweep of *Carnaval*, as well as the inventive writing for the piano, mark it as one of the defining works of the Romantic era.

Cello Concerto in B Minor, op. 104, Antonín Dvořák (1895): During the last of Dvořák's three years in the United States, he composed what is understandably regarded as the greatest concerto for cello and orchestra. It was, at least in part, influenced by the Cello Concerto no. 2 by American composer Victor Herbert, who is much better known for his charming operettas. Dvořák admired both the structural unity and orchestration of the Herbert score, but the new score is all Dvořák. It's more like a grand symphony than a concerto yet, for all the fullness of scale, it can be very intimate.

Dvořák's homesickness for his native Bohemia can be felt in the score; some hear characteristics of American folk music, too (as in his Symphony no. 9, *From the New World*, written two years earlier in the United States). The work is cast in conventional three-movement form, but there is little conventional about what Dvořák does within each of those movements. Themes are ingeniously worked out, passed between cello and orchestra as if in an intent dialogue. Music from the very opening of the concerto returns at the end to provide a satisfying sense of unity to the piece. Throughout, woodwinds, especially the clarinet, are given prominence, their tonal shading providing a perfect counterpart to the cello's mellow quality. The concerto certainly has a bravura side, putting the cellist through some tough paces, but it is the heartfelt element of the music that proves most impressive.

Clarinet Quintet in A Major, K. 581, Wolfgang Amadeus Mozart (1789): For a perfect demonstration of Mozart's ineffable melodies and pure eloquence, you need only listen to his Clarinet Quintet. Written two years before his death, the work is imbued with calmness, perhaps even resignation. The sheer beauty of the writing is striking; Mozart clearly found the combination of clarinet, two violins, a viola, and a cello to be a most congenial one. In addition to the steady flow of poetic themes, the quintet offers a model of instrumental shading and clarity; the five instruments blend with exquisite transparency. One of the other invaluable things about this piece is that it inspired another affecting one— the autumn-tinted Clarinet Quintet by Brahms, written nearly a century later.

Concerto for Orchestra, Béla Bártok (1943, revised 1945): After composing a lot of music brimming with dissonance and often wildly unpredictable rhythms, Bártok unexpectedly moved toward a somewhat simpler style in this, his final masterpiece. Not that the Concerto for Orchestra is simple, not by a long shot. But there is a strong directness to the melodic material which, like nearly all of Bártok's output, has firm roots in Hungarian folk music.

The title of this five-movement work makes plain that the orchestra itself, and various individuals or small groups within it, will fulfill the function of a soloist in a traditional concerto. The wind instruments, for example, get a workout in the second movement, called "Game of Pairs," which offers marvelous subtleties of tone (a snare drum punctuates the movement tellingly). There are passages that require virtuosity from the whole orchestra; the aggressive, invigorating finale is a particularly tough test for an ensemble—and a conductor. Add in moments of nocturnal eeriness (the third movement, "Elegy") and wicked wit (the "Interrupted Intermezzo," with its Bronx cheer from the brass pointedly aimed at another composer, Shostakovich), and the Concerto offers abundant entertainment, as well as musical substance.

The Creation, Joseph Haydn (1798): Although Haydn poured plenty of genius into his more than one hundred symphonies (he was justifiably nicknamed the "Father of the Symphony"), his oratorio *The Creation*, written late in his life and based on the Bible's Book of Genesis, sums up his own flair for creation. The work is scored for vocal soloists, chorus, and orchestra. In the instrumental introduction, Haydn's depiction of the universe being formed out of chaos—strange harmonies gradually resolving into soothing consonance—ranks among the most creative (so to speak) passages in all of classical music.

The score abounds in pictorial touches. When the chorus sings "and there was light," the blazing sound that follows still makes a magical, shattering effect. Evocations of nature are quite literal, from "foaming billows" of the seas (the music rolls up and down like waves) to the appearance of lions on the earth (a brassy roar). In the last passage, Adam (bass soloist) and Eve (soprano) sing of their love for the Creator, but the music warns us of their impending fall from grace when, as the oratorio ends, the harmony takes an understated, downward slide. Such moments explain the exalted status of this oratorio.

Daphnis et Chloe, **Suite no. 2,** Maurice Ravel (1912): The year before the famous riot in Paris provoked by the premiere of a ballet choreographed by Nijinsky with music by Stravinsky, another ballet premiere in Paris, danced by Nijinsky with music by Ravel, provoked a somewhat less incendiary reaction. More like yawns, actually. The plot had to do with a kidnaping by pirates and dramatic rescue in ancient Greece.

Although the ballet failed to make an impression, Ravel salvaged his side of things by fashioning two orchestral suites that could be performed in concert. Suite no. 2, containing the luscious final three scenes of the ballet, became a particular favorite with audiences. No wonder. From the depiction of daybreak (bird calls in the woodwinds and gradually intensifying strings) to the whirling, orgiastic conclusion, the suite presents a veritable textbook of multichromatic orchestration. Ravel's beguiling melodies and exotic harmonies are no less remarkable. This suite, like the entire ballet score, which has become more popular on recordings over the years, provides an unusually sensuous aural experience.

Dichterliebe **("Poet's Love"), op. 48,** Robert Schumann (1840): Like Schubert's *Die schone Mullerin*, this song cycle represents one of the glories of German lieder. The poet is Heinrich Heine, who keenly expressed the ironic side of loves won and lost. Having experienced his own share of romantic ups and downs before wedding his beloved Clara, Schumann felt a connection to Heine's vibrant words.

The sixteen songs in this cycle cover the gamut of feelings awakened by a love affair, from light-headed rhapsody (as in the dreamy opening song about the "lovely month of May") to bitterness (the angry outbursts in *Ich grolle nicht*). Throughout, the writing for the voice is effortless and natural; the piano is an equal partner, reinforcing the words and also communicating much of what is left unsaid by the poetry.

Die schone Mullerin ("The Fair Maid of the Mill"), D. 795, Franz Schubert (1823): Schubert, a master of composing song cycles, composed a perfect example of the genre in *Die schone Mullerin*, based on poetry by Wilhelm Muller. The texts deal with themes dear to the hearts of nineteenth-century Romantics—a wandering loner, unrequited love, and death. The poems don't form so much a traditional plot as a series of vignettes that reveal the soul of the tortured artist trying to forget his beloved maid of the mill, and concluding that peace is most likely to be found in the next life. Despite the bleak outlook, this cycle contains some of the most purely beautiful songs Schubert ever wrote. The piano part is every bit as impressive and effective as the vocal part, allowing us to hear not only such descriptive things as the churning of the mill wheels and the rolling of the stream, but also to sense the psychological state of the forlorn lover.

Don Juan, op. 20, Richard Strauss (1889): It's not easy to single out one Strauss tone poem, since nearly all of them reflect the composer's musical inventiveness and are valued standards of the orchestral repertoire. *Don Juan*, the work of a twenty-four-year-old, is one of the most compact of these works. It demonstrates a surprisingly masterful command of melody and orchestral forces, as well as a knack for dramatic storytelling through music.

The Don Juan portrayed here is not quite the same man from Mozart's celebrated opera *Don Giovanni*; Strauss took as his guide a poem by Nikolaus Lenau, which gives us more of an idealist than an amoralist. The composer provides a taut, ear-grabbing introduction to the character and, later, in one of the most glorious themes ever written, has the horns reveal the intensity of the Don's libido. A rapturous oboe solo is among the other highlights in the score, which ends not with a bang, but an intriguing whisper.

Enigma **Variations, op. 36,** Edward Elgar (1899): The formal title of this engaging work, *Variations on an Original Theme*, only tells part of the tale. Sir Edward Elgar made things a little more complicated—more enigmatic. There may really be two themes being subjected to variations in this score—the "original theme," clearly heard at the beginning, and another theme that Elgar said was going through the whole piece, but never actually played. People argue to this day whether there really is a second theme (all sorts of suggestions have been made as to what it is), or whether Elgar really meant something symbolic, such as the theme of friendship. It's also possible that he was just pulling everyone's leg.

To be sure, friendship is the overriding point of the score. Each of the fourteen variations is a portrait in sound of one of the composer's friends, identified only by initials or nicknames.

Sometimes, the results are delectably evocative. "Variation XI," for example, is dedicated to an organist friend of Elgar's who had a bulldog; you can easily hear the pet fall into a river and splash his way back out. "Variation XIII" recalls a lady friend departing on an ocean voyage, complete with the rumble of the ship's engines. "Variation IX," known as *Nimrod*, is a tribute to Elgar's publisher, and also one of the composer's noblest ideas. Although the personal allusions enhance enjoyment of the *Enigma* Variations, the score stands solidly on its own purely musical grounds as one of the most accomplished works in the symphonic repertoire.

The Four Seasons, Antonio Vivaldi (1725): This is one of the first substantial cases of music that conveys a specific story or idea. Although such program music would become a major manifestation of nineteenth-century Romanticism, it was very rare in the Baroque era. Vivaldi produced a sequence of four violin concertos, each with the standard three movements of the time (fast, slow, fast), that correspond to the seasons of the year. For each concerto, Vivaldi provided a very detailed sonnet (he probably was the poet) that describes the season at hand both in general and in quite detailed terms. His music puts into sound all sorts of poetic images—a dog barking in *Spring*; the draining heat and annoying flies of *Summer*; an *Autumn* hunt; people stamping their feet in the cold and gingerly walking on ice in *Winter*.

It is possible to forget all about these poems and these incidents and simply drink in the flow of memorable melodies and pictorial effects of each concerto. Either way, *The Four Seasons* represents a high point in Vivaldi's output.

Goldberg Variations, Johann Sebastian Bach (1741): The name of this composition requires explanation. Johann Gottlieb Goldberg, a pupil of Bach's, was a keyboard player in the employ of Count Keyselingk, who reportedly suffered from insomnia. The old, probably apocryphal story goes that the count commissioned Bach to write an extended harpsichord piece to be played by Goldberg during sleepless nights. Whatever the real circumstances were, Bach certainly produced a monument to the musical form known as "theme and variations."

Bach's theme is called here an "aria," reflecting its songlike characteristic. After it is played through, Bach offers thirty variations on it, each one more ingenious than the last, but always clearly related to the aria's harmonic progression and various aspects of the melody's contour so that the ear remains connected in some way to the foundation of the piece. Making things more intriguing is that the variations are presented in groups of three, with the third one always in the form of a "canon." The final variation is a "quodlibet," with two popular tunes of the day (one of them called "Cabbage and Turnips") being used as fresh counterpoint to the aria's harmonic pattern. Finally, the aria is reprised, bringing the listener back to the starting point and providing a sense of resolution and fulfillment.

Harmonielehre, John Adams (1985): Even listeners who ordinarily find the style known as minimalism extremely annoying have been won over by the sheer emotive force of this orchestral score. Prompted by some strange dreams Adams had (including one of a huge tanker lifting up out of San Francisco Bay and soaring skyward), *Harmonielehre* takes its name from the title of a 1911 treatise on harmony by Arnold Schoenberg, the composer who went on to lead the atonal revolution. Adams takes the lush harmonies of Romanticism and gives them a fresh workout in an expansive, mesmerizing manner.

Cast in three movements, *Harmonielehre* has as its central movement a brooding reflection called "The Amfortas Wound," referring to a character in Richard Wagner's mystical opera *Parsifal* who has a wound that cannot be healed. The music here recalls not just Wagner, but Mahler in its intensity. The two outer movements are propelled by the reiterative rhythmic patterns associated with minimalism, here given terrific boldness by Adams's prismatic orchestration.

La Mer, Claude Debussy (1905): This large orchestral score is one of the composer's most ambitious and, it can be argued, most brilliant. Inspired by the work of Japanese printmaker Katsushika Hokusai, *La Mer* is an extended tone poem about the sea. (Debussy subtitled the work "Three Symphonic Sketches.")

There are specific descriptions to each movement—"From dawn until noon on the sea," "Play of the waves," "Dialogue of the wind and the sea." The music conveys those images with masterly strokes of sound; the evocation of sunrise in the first sketch is particularly atmospheric. The orchestration is superb; Debussy could get out of the same instruments of Brahms and Wagner an entirely different prism of sounds, from the gentlest to the most blazing, that those composers could never have conjured. The painterly effects and Debussy's unique style of harmony, reinforcing his reputation as an Impressionist, combine to produce an almost magical effect with all the nuances of a Renoir canvas.

Messiah, George Frideric Handel (1741): Too often, this oratorio is performed incomplete, so many people have only a partial understanding of what makes it so valuable. There's certainly a lot more to this score than the "Hallelujah!" chorus. Unlike some other Handel oratorios, which are closer to opera in terms of dramatic narrative, *Messiah* (there is no "the" in the title) is mostly a reflective piece, using texts from the Old and New Testaments. The score is in three parts, offering an extended contemplation on the meaning of Jesus' life and death. "Part the First" is concerned primarily with the Nativity, "Part the Second" with the suffering of Jesus, "Part the Third" with resurrection and the last judgment.

Handel's use of counterpoint here is superb; he gets maximum musical mileage out of a four-part chorus—sopranos, altos, tenors, and basses—by weaving their lines together to summon all sorts of vivid effects. And throughout there is marvelous "word-painting," when the melodic line mirrors the meaning of the words. One example: the up-and-down notes whenever the tenor soloist sings the word *crooked* in the "Ev'ry Valley" aria. The orchestral writing is no less pictorial; note the high, shimmering violins that convey the fluttering of wings when the angels appear before the shepherds. And there are telling theatrical effects, too, among them having the chorus suddenly go from barely audible at the line "Since by man came death" to downright explosive at the next line, "By man came also the resurrection of the dead." The solo arias offer abundant possibilities for embellishment.

That Handel himself was a believer can be heard in every measure of the oratorio; the score exudes an inner faith. In purely musical terms, *Messiah* exudes an astonishing artistic vitality.

Overture to *A Midsummer Night's Dream*, Felix Mendelssohn (1826): Mendelssohn was all of seventeen when his love of Shakespeare generated this luminous piece. It was not originally intended to be an overture to anything, but rather a single-movement evocation of *A Midsummer Night's Dream*. (Another seventeen years later, the composer was asked to provide incidental music to a production of the play; he added several more evocative items to complement this overture, including the *Wedding March* that has accompanied many a bride and groom down the aisle since.)

The overture begins and ends with deliciously evocative chords from the woodwinds that place the listener immediately into the fairy realm of the play. There is more enchantment from the violins, which are used in a way that no one previously had conceived; Mendelssohn makes the instruments sound elfin and ethereal. It's pure musical magic. And so is the rest of this charm-spinning overture, which even manages to evoke the hee-hawing of a donkey—a reminder of what happens to the character of Bottom in the comedy.

Piano Concerto no. 2 in B-flat Major, op. 83, Johannes Brahms (1881): With his typical wit, Brahms described this as "a little concerto," but it actually lasts longer than any of his four symphonies. It is, in many ways, a kind of symphony for piano and orchestra. Rather than the usual three movements of a concerto (including Brahms's dramatic Piano Concerto no. 1 in D Minor), there are four movements, as in a symphony.

The B-flat Major Concerto requires sterling virtuosity from a pianist, but also tenderness and, in the finale, good humor. From the opening horn theme (one of the most inviting musical entrances anyone ever composed), to the bold scherzo, to the sublime duet for cello and piano in the third movement, to the gently rollicking finale, the concerto captures Brahms at his most congenial. The interaction between piano and orchestra in this piece constitutes a multilayered, ever-involving dialogue.

Piano Concerto no. 3 in D Minor, op. 30, Sergei Rachmaninoff (1909): It did not take the 1996 hit movie *Shine* to affirm the quality and challenge of this concerto, which became the primary musical protagonist in the film. The score has long been prized by pianists, drawn to its almost solemn beauty and virtuosic keyboard writing. Although Rachmaninoff's soaring Piano Concerto no. 2 is the more popular work, the Third rises somewhat above it in terms of breadth and expressive content. This is not just a vehicle for an accomplished pianist, nor just a treasure of indelible tunes; this is the last Romantic—in the fullest sense of the word—piano concerto.

The soloist's brooding opening theme, supported by a subdued, seemingly anxious orchestra, sets in motion a tense drama that does not really find release until the headlong rush of the concerto's closing measures.

Piano Concerto no. 20 in D Minor, K. 466, Wolfgang Amadeus Mozart (1785): At least a dozen of Mozart's twenty-seven piano concertos are among the most finely crafted, not to mention eventful, works ever written for piano and orchestra; they are often like miniopéras, the themes serving as characters. In the case of this D Minor Concerto, it's like a very dramatic opera. (It's worth noting that the key of D Minor is the same key used in the final scene of *Don Giovanni*, when the antihero descends into hell.)

There is considerable force and urgency behind the concerto's first movement, presaging Beethoven, who patterned his Piano Concerto no. 3 after this piece. The middle movement, which

Mozart called a *Romanze* (no wonder the Romantics in the next century embraced this concerto so strongly), alternates between sublime poetry and temporary storm clouds; the finale resumes the tense mood of the opening, only to be hit with a redemptive blaze of sunny D Major to help bring the curtain down on this wordless drama.

Piano Sonata in B Minor, Franz Liszt (1853): In a way, nearly everything Liszt composed was daring. He wrote music as he lived life—unconventionally. With this sonata, Liszt revealed his grasp of form and thematic development, two essential ingredients of classical music. The piece is about thirty uninterrupted minutes long. It can be heard as a one-movement work that loosely follows the traditional "sonata form" structure, but it also can be heard as four movements laid out like a grand symphony. It's all in the ear of the listener.

Adding to the ingenuity of this audacious sonata is the wonderfully pliable nature of Liszt's themes. They are derived from a few short, melodic seeds that appear early on in the work and generate myriad harmonies, not to mention episodes of drama, passion, poetry, and reflection. The result is a kind of continual organic growth, starting and ending with the same hushed notes of uncertainty and expectancy. The B Minor Sonata boldly reflects the spirit of Romanticism.

Piano Sonata no. 23 in F Minor, op. 57 *(Appassionata),* Ludwig van Beethoven (1805): Beethoven's thirty-two Piano Sonatas contain an unparalleled range of feeling, tone coloring, technical challenges, and sheer creativity. Virtually any of the sonatas have much to offer the Curious Listener, from the famous *Moonlight* Sonata, with its hushed, totally unprecedented opening movement, to the last sonatas, with their unpredictable forms and daring harmonies.

The *Appassionata* Sonata is well-nicknamed, for it is propelled by an almost overwhelming passion. It also presents a formidable test of a pianist's technique, calling for dramatic rushes up and down the keyboard and massive sonorities in the first and third movements; an understated touch in the serene, rather noble middle movement (a set of variations on a theme). Incidentally, the sonata shares not only something of the Fifth Symphony's energy, but even makes use, in the first movement, of the same four-note pattern that starts that symphony.

Prelude and *Liebestod* from *Tristan und Isolde*, Richard Wagner (1859): The crusty nineteenth-century Viennese critic Eduard Hanslick declared that the Prelude to Wagner's most sensuous opera, *Tristan und Isolde*, reminded him of a "painting of a martyr whose intestines are slowly unwound from his body on a reel." Hanslick wasn't the only learned listener who could not grasp the daring and almost mystical beauty of what Wagner had achieved in this single orchestral passage.

Frequently played out of its original context, the Prelude took all of what was known up to that time about Western harmony and led it into unchartered territory. Richer chords, full of uncertainty and expectancy, replaced the simpler, more predictable progressions that had long served composers from Bach through Brahms. The melodic line above those chords is likewise very different; it refuses to go in the direction the tradition-laden ear expects it to go, but keeps twisting around itself, like those intestines.

Wagner holds all of these bold ideas together ingeniously in a seamless piece of music that never finds a comfort zone but is forever seeking consummation, a sonic home. In the opera, a pair of doomed lovers is also forever seeking consummation. That relief occurs only at the very end of the opera, in the ecstatic, soul-stirring *Liebestod* ("Love-Death"), which is often performed without the vocal part as an orchestral companion to the Prelude.

It is impossible to overstate the importance of the Prelude—indeed, the very first chord that occurs in that piece (it's still called the *Tristan* chord)—to the history of classical music. It fueled the Romantic movement and led the way into many new directions. These opening and closing passages of *Tristan*, the musical embodiment of longing and fulfillment, continue to cast a spell on performers and listeners alike.

Prelude to the Afternoon of a Faun, Claude Debussy (1894): A rather dense poem by Stéphane Mallarmé triggered what is perhaps Debussy's most famous work. It evokes a mythological scene, with a faun awakening from sleep, yearning for a nymph and sinking back into slumber. There is an erotic element to the scenario, which was famously exploited by the legendary dancer Nijinsky when he danced to this music.

None of that imagery needs to concern the listener; the music can be experienced in a totally abstract way. But there is no getting around the sensual undercurrent of the score, which gives it a unique flavor. When it was new, the music seemed almost revolutionary, its delicately applied orchestral hues producing an effect unlike anything else being written at the time. From the opening, languorous flute solo, the ear is drawn into an exquisite dreamscape. This is misty music, filled with subtly exotic turns of phrase and harmony. In the space of only about ten minutes, Debussy's tone poem is as eventful and riveting as the longest, splashiest ones of Richard Strauss.

Rhapsody in Blue, George Gershwin (1924): On the night of Feb. 12, 1924, New York's Aeolian Hall was filled with an audience drawn to "An Experiment in Modern Music." At the end of a long program that hadn't been terribly modern up to that point, an unsuspecting audience was suddenly jolted by the wild clarinet riff that opens *Rhapsody in Blue.* Ears and minds were blown open.

Hastily written for that New York concert, the piece successfully brought the exuberance and earthiness of jazz into a formal concert hall setting. It demonstrated, especially, the communicative power of jazz rhythms. Gershwin's typically sparkling piano writing also gives the score character, as does his ability to unleash a delicious melody. The big tune of the *Rhapsody*, which appears more than halfway through, has been a part of the public consciousness almost since that first performance.

Requiem, Gabriel Fauré (1877, revised 1887–1900): Prior to this work, most settings of the ancient Latin Mass for the Dead emphasized horror and fear of the last judgment. Fauré set out to provide something more consoling. His Requiem largely dispenses with references to flaming pits and brimstone. Instead, Fauré evokes an aura of peace and hope, nowhere more poignantly than in the *Pie Jesu* for soprano solo.

Throughout the Requiem, Fauré uses chorus, soprano, and baritone soloists and orchestra with a superb sense of aural coloring (because he worked on the score for two decades there are different versions; the commonly performed edition for full orchestra dates from 1900). As pure music, the piece represents a major contribution to the French repertoire and a work of art that can speak to listeners of any (or no) faith on a very personal level in unusually comforting, enriching ways.

Requiem, Giuseppe Verdi (1874): In addition to being Italy's most illustrious opera composer, Verdi was also one of its most valued patriots, whose fervent desire to see an Italy unified and free of foreign domination was reflected in various ways through his music. Another leading voice for these causes was poet Alessandro Manzoni, whose death greatly affected Verdi. The composer's sorrow found a soul-stirring outlet in the form of a Requiem for four vocal soloists, chorus, and orchestra. Sometimes referred to as "The Manzoni Requiem," this grandly scaled score was never intended to be a part of a church service; it is strictly a concert work. Verdi himself was not a religious man in any conventional sense, but something in the text of the ancient Latin Mass for the Dead spoke to him in an unusually forceful way.

This Requiem is as much for the living as for the dead. Genuine terrors are conjured up in the hair-raising *Dies Irae* ("Day of Judgment") section, with its furiously pounding bass drum and screaming brass; this movement takes up nearly half the whole work. There are more comforting passages as well, including the tender *Salve me* and *Lacrimosa.* And there are several solos of operatic proportion, including the rapturous *Ingemisco* for tenor and the Requiem's concluding *Libera me*, which has the soprano pleading for salvation in a chilling, dramatic manner. For its stunning originality and emotional pull, Verdi's Requiem is one of the crowning works not just of sacred music, but of all music.

The Rite of Spring, Igor Stravinsky (1913): There hasn't been a good riot in a theater since this ballet was first performed. It's easy to understand how the music coming from the orchestra pit proved too much to take for some in the audience at the premiere of *The Rite of Spring*. It is a brutal, bracing, brilliant score. From the first primordial mutterings and unsettled sounds by the wind instruments, suggesting a strange and ancient landscape, to the final frenzied moments, when the senses are almost bruised by the percussive orgy of the ritual dance, the music exerts a magnetic hold.

Stravinsky's groundbreaking use of multiple rhythms—the number of beats per measure changes constantly in some sections—served as a kind of musical liberation, a defiant break from traditional symmetry. His orchestration expanded on all of the effects that were traditional in late-nineteenth-century Russian music and devised a whole new aural dimension; instruments had never been used quite so daringly before—low, snarling woodwinds, biting brass, and stark, aggressive strings. Dissonance, though not full atonality, is the normal language of this score, but Stravinsky makes that language, in its own way, as logical and communicative as Mozart's melodic style. *The Rite of Spring* still sounds fresh and revolutionary today, another sign of the mastery behind it.

Romeo and Juliet, Sergei Prokofiev (1938): Like the ballet scores of Tchaikovsky, Prokofiev's music for a ballet based on the tragedy of Shakespeare's most famous lovers enjoys an active concert life on its own. Prokofiev formed two suites out of the complete score, made up of various scenes that do not neces sarily follow the story line; Suite no. 2 is the more dramatically effective. It has become common for conductors to put together their own suites for concerts and recordings.

Prokofiev poured into this ballet some of his most lyrical and pictorial music, as well as some of his most visceral ("The Death of Tybalt," a stunning showpiece for orchestra, packs a particular punch). For its color and virtuosity, its wealth of melody, *Romeo and Juliet* exemplifies Prokofiev's creative spark.

St. Matthew Passion, Johann Sebastian Bach (1727): In this musical setting of the St. Matthew gospel and additional, reflective texts, Bach emphasizes the suffering of Jesus, and the human failings and fears of his followers and persecutors. The result is a work of sweeping drama and deep reflection that ultimately transcends any religious dogma.

It is a large-scale work—five vocal soloists, two choruses, two orchestras, two organs, and a harpsichord. There is almost an operatic quality to the music, with solo arias and choral numbers generating a strong, dramatic flow. A tenor soloist serves as the Evangelist, fulfilling the function of narrator; a bass soloist sings the words of Jesus; other soloists represent Peter, Judas, and Pilate; the choruses depict the crowds turning against Jesus and also represent the present-day congregation contemplating the meaning of the story. Running through the *Passion* is a chorale tune that gets harmonized with increasing complexity as the events themselves get more complex. The music continuously reinforces the words, sometimes to great pictorial effect, so that Peter's weeping or the rending of the temple veil can easily be visualized. The personal commitment behind the notes is as impressive as the sophistication of Bach's melodic and harmonic ideas, his orchestration, and his organizational skill. The *St. Matthew Passion* stands as a monument to the composer, his faith, and the art of Baroque music.

String Quartet in C Major, op. 76, no. 3 *(Emperor)*, Joseph Haydn (1797): The combination of two violins, viola, and cello proved to be a magnet for Haydn; the sureness of technique and elegance of expression in his many quartets remain the benchmark for the idiom. The *Emperor* Quartet typifies Haydn's mastery of form and content. Each of the four movements is full of character, but it is the second one that stands out—and provides the work with its nickname. This movement consists of exceedingly eloquent variations on a noble hymn Haydn had written earlier and which served as the Austrian national anthem (unfortunately, later associated with Nazi Germany).

String Quartet in F Major, Maurice Ravel (1903): For sheer quality of texture—transparent, silken threads of sound—this quartet is hard to beat. But there is much more to it than that. Ravel's ingratiating themes are developed with flair, and his superb writing for the instruments coaxes a prism of tones.

It is hard to believe that Ravel wrote it when he was still a student, the work boasts such assurance and ripe imagination. Although he would later avoid some of the old musical forms handed down from the German side of classical music (Mozart, Haydn, Beethoven, and so on), Ravel showed perfect control of traditional sonata form in the first movement. There's a traditional, three-part scherzo movement, too. But Ravel takes these venerable structures and makes them his own with lush harmonies and multiple aural effects, yielding a work of subtle sensuality.

String Quartet no. 4, Béla Bártok (1928): Bártok's six string quartets, each with its own character, represent a high-water mark of twentieth-century music. No. 4 commands particular attention for the ingenuity of its structure and the vitality of thematic material. The score suggests a taut, five-act drama. Bártok, a master of design, fashions a perfectly symmetrical model, placing the foundation of the quartet at the center—a foggy sort of night music that serves as the third movement. The second and fourth movements are propulsive scherzos with related melodic material; the first and fifth movements are also fast and also related to each other thematically. All sorts of provocative sound effects add to the picture—glissandos in the second movement, pizzicato playing in the fourth—but it is the intent behind such effects that gives this quartet its lasting power.

String Quintet in C Major, D. 956, Franz Schubert (1828): Only two months before he died, Schubert wrote what many consider to be his richest work of chamber music. His reservoir of melodic ideas supplied him with unforgettable themes to build upon, while his sense of structural cohesion allowed him to build a grand structure to house and develop those themes.

The choice of instrumentation was significant in itself. Where Mozart had added a second viola to the standard string quartet of two violins, viola, and cello to form a string quintet, Schubert used another cello as the fifth player. This meant a darker color to the sound and also seemed to generate an extra degree of lyricism, as when the two cellos practically sing the tender second theme of the first movement. It is tempting to assume that Schubert wrote the Quintet fully aware of his mortality, for a certain bittersweetness haunts much of the score, and even the dashing finale seems to have a shadow hovering over it. This is Schubert at his most revealing and moving.

Suites for Solo Cello, Johann Sebastian Bach (c. 1720): If there is a musical equivalent for the source of the Nile, these six suites would be a good choice. The same could be said for the six works Bach wrote around the same time for solo violin. In both cases, he revealed not only awesome compositional technique, but the very soul of the musical art, using nothing more than a single instrument with four strings.

Each suite has six movements, starting with a prelude and proceeding through five of the typical dance forms of Baroque music, yet each suite has its own characteristics, from incandescence to joviality to intense sorrow. Although often performed separately, the cello suites have come to be viewed as a totality, a summation of Bach's craft and sensibilities. The music tests a cellist's powers of expression as much as physical skills; such intimate works as these will reveal everything about an artist, just as they reveal so much of Bach's mind and heart.

Symphonie fantastique, Hector Berlioz (1830): A symphony about drug use may seem an unlikely prospect for an honored work of musical art, but listening to *Symphonie fantastique* need not compromise anyone's moral standards. After unsuccessfully pursuing a mediocre English actress who performed with a Shakespearean troupe in Paris, Berlioz came up with a wild idea to work out his frustration. He devised a scenario about an unhappy man who, crushed by a woman's indifference, takes opium and begins to hallucinate some good and bad things about her.

He begins by remembering his beloved at her ideal best— she is represented by a theme in the orchestra that will come back continually, a device Berlioz called an *idee fixe* (fixed idea). Then we are at a grand ball, where he and the beloved dance blissfully. Next, our lovesick gentleman is out in the country alone, thinking about her; the orchestra tells us, by means of giving her theme a murky tint, that she is not being faithful to him. So, by the next movement, he has killed her, an act that gets him executed to the shattering sounds of the "March to the Scaffold." Just as the guillotine is to fall, the return of the *idee fixe* tells us he is thinking once more of her; the blade cuts off that final reminiscence. The opium really goes into effect then, for our hero next imagines himself at a witches' Sabbath, with his beloved as the head witch (the *idee fixe* now sounds distorted and decidedly wicked).

Behind this crazy story is music of brazen individuality. The orchestration alone is special; it would influence composers for generations to come. And the way Berlioz holds the five movements together by means of the recurring theme would likewise serve as a valued model in the future. Even if you knew nothing about the plot behind the notes, the music can still grab you by the ear and never let go. By the way, a few years after the premiere of the symphony, that English actress decided to reconsider the composer's advances and marry him, but the union turned out to be anything but fantastique.

Symphony no. 1, John Corigliano (1990): Having lost many friends to the AIDS epidemic, Corigliano was moved to write this memorial, which also serves as a manifesto of rage against the disease, the indifference of governments to its toll, and the bigotry of society toward those infected with it. This confrontational aspect of the 1990 symphony, and the flood of emotions behind the notes, made some listeners uncomfortable when it was introduced, but the work won over most of the public; before the decade was out, it had received performances by more than one hundred orchestras around the world, an enviable record for any piece of new music.

A single note, sounded in unison and gradually built up in volume to a shattering level, begins the symphony and returns toward the end, suggesting an uncontrollable wail. References to Corigliano's friends are woven throughout the score. In the first movement, an off-stage piano plays the popular "Tango" by Isaac Albeniz, a favorite piece of a pianist who was dying as the symphony was being composed. The second movement, a fierce scherzo, alternates between a giddy tarantella (the Italian folk dance said to be danced by victims of poisonous spider bites) and horrifying, chaotic outbursts, suggesting the dementia suffered by another friend. The third movement remembers two cellists with a haunting duet. All of this material returns in the "Epilogue," tempered by wave after wave of soft, brass chords that suggest a kind of peace for the dead and the living alike. The symphony is one of the most provocative, affecting scores to come out of the twentieth century.

Symphony no. 1 in C Minor, op. 68, Johannes Brahms (1876): It took Brahms more than twenty years to finish his first symphony. No wonder. Beethoven's nine symphonies were a tough act to follow, even half a century after that composer's death. In a way, it seems that Brahms finally decided if you can't beat 'em, join 'em—or at least appropriate some of their best ideas. So his symphony incorporates aspects of Beethoven's Fifth and Ninth, which explains why some wags dubbed it "Beethoven's Tenth." But this is very definitely an original achievement.

The legacy of Beethoven is felt, above all, in the dramatic outline of the symphony—the way it progresses from the darkness of C minor in the first movement to the radiance of C major in the last (just as in Beethoven's Fifth). There's also a fascinating melodic connection; the grand theme that emerges in the finale bears an unmistakable resemblance to the *Ode to Joy* tune from Beethoven's Ninth.

Too much can be made of these likenesses, for it is the tone and character of Brahms's First, the richness of ideas, development, and orchestration, that make it stand squarely on its own. The two middle movements could have come only from Brahms; they have a lightness of touch and calmness-before-the-storm nature that is thoroughly beguiling. There also is a wonderful level of tension in the outer movements; the buildup to that famous finale theme creates an edge-of-your-seat suspense, rewarded with a calming burst of sunshine.

Symphony no. 4, Charles Ives (c. 1918): This symphony represents a synthesis of all that made Ives unique. Like his earlier work *The Unanswered Question*, the score does a lot of asking, seeking, and hoping. There are assorted responses, some humorous, some confusing, some religious, and none conclusive. Taken just as pure music, the Fourth Symphony is an astonishing achievement, a kind of testament to artistic pioneering. The fact that it usually takes more than one conductor to hold it all together says a lot. Scored for chorus and huge orchestra, the symphony puts as many demands on performers as it does on listeners.

American audiences have an advantage here. They will recognize many of the snippets of hymns, folk tunes, sentimental ballads, and patriotic songs that pop up, often out of a maze of themes and harmonies (Ives used this technique of musical quotations in many of his works). It is an old hymn that opens and closes the vast symphony ("Bethany"), and another that makes a haunting appearance in the first movement ("Watchman Tell Us of the Night"). A quixotic second movement, which piles on all sorts of allusions to vintage popular music, and a solemn fugue, which ends with a curious snippet of "Joy to the World," are followed by a finale that suggests the passive continuum of time and the perpetual expectancy of faith. There was nothing in American music like this symphony before Ives, and nothing like it since.

Symphony no. 5 in C Minor, op. 67, Ludwig van Beethoven (1808): The first four notes of this symphony are perhaps the best-known in the world; people with no other knowledge of classical music are apt to have those four notes packed somewhere into their subconscious. Over the years, this unifying, four-note motto theme of Beethoven's Fifth has taken on a significance that would have surprised him. In World War II, the notes, corresponding to Morse code for the letter "V," became a symbol of victory for the Allies. Even in Beethoven's time, people began to hear much more than notes in that emphatic da-da-da-DUM. When it was reported that Beethoven himself described the theme as "Thus Fate knocks at the door," everyone believed it. (The composer probably did not say that, but it's too good an image to ignore.)

Four notes alone could not explain this symphony's hold on the imagination, of course. It's what Beethoven does with those notes that counts. His tense, emotion-charged score is held to-gether in large measure by the rhythmic pattern of the motto. You can find that sequence—three short notes, one long—all over the symphony, a common thread holding everything together.

But the dramatic "plot" of the symphony also gives the work uncommon stature. It's not a plot in any conventional sense; this is not a symphony with a clear-cut program, like Beethoven's Sixth, with its depiction of a visit to the country. Yet it's easy to sense a progression in the Fifth, a journey of the heart. The symphony begins with urgency and upheaval, moves momentarily into calmer territory, returns to shadows and mystery, then finally reaches sunlight, exultation, and triumph. This is music abstract on one level, personal and emotional on another. No one before Beethoven had conceived of a musical fusion on such a scale.

Symphony no. 5 in D Minor, op. 47, Dmitri Shostakovich (1937): When Shostakovich ran afoul of Stalin with his provocative opera *Lady Macbeth of Mtsensk* in 1936, his life—not just artistic life—was in jeopardy. Officially condemned for assorted offenses against music, Shostakovich responded the next year with his Fifth Symphony, which was given a subtitle (possibly by the composer himself): "A Soviet artist's response to just criticism." The new work helped bring him back into favor with the state. But the composer was hardly bowing down.

Shostakovich wrote a symphony that could be appreciated on one level as pure music that progresses from sad to happy; this is how unimaginative government types heard it, proclaiming its virtues. On another level, the symphony expresses fear, bitterness, irony, lamentation and, in the end, forced enthusiasm—

a depiction of life under Stalin. The fact that many in the first audience wept openly attests to the possibility of the hidden meaning. The symphony has many echoes of Mahler's sound-world, especially in the scherzo, which recalls Mahler's combination of rustic, songful, and ominous moods. The third movement, a profoundly affecting adagio, is also on a par with Mahler's art. The mock heroics of the finale become uplifting and chilling at the same time.

Symphony no. 6 in B Minor, op. 74 (*Pathetique*), Peter Ilyich Tchaikovsky (1893): It was inevitable that many people would believe that Tchaikovsky wrote this symphony with his own death in mind. After all, he himself labeled it *Pathetique*; it ends with a solemn, sorrow-laden hush; and the composer died a few days after the premiere. But Tchaikovsky was apparently in very good spirits while composing his Sixth Symphony. If this was not his intended swan song, he certainly meant it to be different and provocative; not surprisingly, the reception for the symphony's premiere was quite chilly. But when it was played again a few weeks later, right after his death, it was heard in a completely new light and hailed as a masterpiece.

The dramatic first movement has a searing impact. The blithely off-kilter second movement—it seems to be a waltz, but has five beats to the measure, instead of a waltz's three—makes a perfect metaphor for how Tchaikovsky, a sometimes self-tortured gay man and defiantly individualistic artist, marched to the beat of a different drummer all his life. The third movement actually is a march, one with an almost maniacal urgency and drive. No one had ended a symphony with a slow movement before; Tchaikovsky's radical choice was perhaps his most inspired touch. This finale includes a heart-wrenching melody, which gradually subsides into nothingness; a soft gong just before the end suggests the departure of a soul from the body.

Symphony no. 8 in B Minor, D. 759 *(Unfinished),* Franz Schubert (1822): Like the armless *Venus de Milo,* this incomplete symphony has achieved exalted status. It has not been firmly established exactly why Schubert never wrote a third and fourth movement for this work. It may be that he simply couldn't summon the inspiration. But since he went on to write another full symphony—one of his most ambitious and most satisfying (no. 9, called *The Great*), there is no question that Schubert's muse had not run dry.

Perhaps he just wasn't comfortable continuing down the path he had started for himself with the two movements that he did complete. They are among his most introspective thoughts; the music, especially the introduction section of the first movement, suggests a very private sorrow. The famous, easily hummable theme that soon emerges brings some sunlight into the picture, but not for long; an air of melancholy hangs over even this ingratiating melody. Many listeners hear in the *Unfinished* Symphony the early flowering of the Romantic era in music. To be sure, the highly personal level of expression and the interior drama in this score are quite unlike anything written before.

Symphony no. 9 in D Major, Gustav Mahler (1909): After the death of his daughter and the diagnosis of his own threatening heart disease, Mahler became, in his music at least, obsessed with issues of mortality. In essence, he wrote a trilogy of farewell to this life—Symphony no. 9, *Das Lied von der Erde* ("Song of the Earth," for two vocal soloists and orchestra), and an unfinished Symphony no. 10. There is in each of these works a sense of resignation, sometimes balanced, as in his Ninth Symphony, with bitter irony.

Like Tchaikovsky's last symphony, the *Pathetique*, which also deals with farewell and letting go, Mahler's Ninth opens and closes with an achingly slow movement; in between come a curious waltz and an eerie, often violent march. The level of profundity achieved by Mahler in this work has never really been surpassed. The ebbing away of sound at the very end is as close as we are likely to get to a musical evocation of what it means to slip past the last threads of this life into the unknown beyond.

Symphony no. 9 in D Minor, op. 125 (*Choral*), Ludwig van Beethoven (1824): As in the Fifth Symphony, there is no question that a musical drama is taking place within the four-movement structure of the Ninth. Again, there is a journey that leads from night to light, from uncertainty to certainty. And, as he had done with his Third Symphony, Beethoven made a significant statement in terms of length alone; there had never been such a long symphony before. It was not just a matter of length that made it so unusual, but a matter of content. In the last movement, Beethoven added human voices for the first time in a symphony—four soloists and a chorus. The shock of that novelty lasted for decades; some timid souls thought Beethoven had gone too far. But, over time, the Ninth was recognized as a monumental achievement, a demonstration of extraordinary originality and expressive depth.

Although the choral finale, with its stirring words about brotherhood, is the chief attention-grabber (the text is the *Ode to Joy* by the German poet Schiller), the rest of the symphony has just as much to offer. In the first movement you can visualize the universe emerging out of an unfathomable void; the second movement's explosive energy suggests a vast cosmic struggle; the third movement reveals the soul of lyricism and, perhaps, of Beethoven himself.

Symphony no. 9 in D Minor, Anton Bruckner (1894): The curse of no. 9 seems to have haunted quite a few composers who tried to match or better Beethoven's total of symphonies—Dvořák, Mahler, and Vaughan Williams are among those who never got all the way to (or all the way through) a no. 10. Bruckner knew he wouldn't make it; it is said that he was working feverishly on the finale to his Ninth Symphony on the day he died. Although he was not able to finish the finale, he left a work that feels complete.

The three completed movements form a summation of Bruckner's unusual art; the second movement exemplifies his trademark way of writing a scherzo, with a hypnotic beat and blazing brass. His symphonies often suggest vast cathedrals in sound, built with a series of broad themes in each movement, like huge stones forming a spire. A devout Catholic, Bruckner could achieve a rare spirituality in his music, nowhere more compellingly than in what turned out to be the last movement of the Ninth Symphony—a solemn, yet uplifting adagio that contains, fittingly, quotations of a few melodies from Bruckner's own settings of the Catholic Mass.

Symphony no. 40 in G Minor, K. 550, Wolfgang Amadeus Mozart (1788): One of the few symphonies Mozart wrote in a minor key, no. 40 used to be viewed as having a tragic undertone, reflecting terrible angst in the composer's psyche. Scholarship has determined that Mozart couldn't have been much jollier at the time the symphony was written. So much for Freudian analysis. But the fact remains that this work does have an extraordinarily dramatic dimension, built right into the urgent theme that launches the first movement. That's only part of its appeal, though.

Mozart's genius for organizing and developing melodic material is evident everywhere in this symphony, from that propulsive opening to the poetic andante movement and the rather grim minuet. In the gripping finale, Mozart reinforces the sense of brooding, driving force from the first movement to put the finishing touch on the score.

Symphony of Psalms, Igor Stravinsky (1930): In the mid-1920s, the previously unreligious Stravinsky decided to embrace the pre-Revolution faith of his native country, the Russian Orthodox Church. This haunting work for chorus and orchestra, based on biblical psalms, subtly reflects that faith; this is not a preachy piece.

The orchestration alone is fascinating—violins and violas are eliminated, leaving a predominantly dark instrumental foundation for the singers. The style of the music is far removed from the composer's *The Rite of Spring* astringency; the work contains some of Stravinsky's most comforting, almost luscious harmonies. The way he sets the word *Alleluia* is a prime illustration; the heartfelt nature of the phrase is like the sun suddenly breaking through threatening clouds.

Twenty-Four Preludes, op. 28, Frederic Chopin (1839): Like Bach's epic *The Well-Tempered Clavier,* a collection of preludes and fugues in every key, Chopin's Preludes cover all the major and minor keys—C major, C minor, D major, D minor, etc. (But there is no fugue to complement each prelude.) Each of these preludes can be played by itself, out of context, as a musical snapshot; it was Chopin who first demonstrated that although the term *prelude* implies an introduction to something else, it can be an independent, free-form thought. But when played in succession, these twenty-four pieces, with their variety of ideas—brief or extended, sweet or explosive, quixotic or straightforward—add up to a remarkably cohesive, compelling experience.

Chopin's seemingly limitless ideas about keyboard coloring yield some amazing results here, and also provide a kind of summation of his style. The concise, supremely elegant waltz that forms the A-Major Prelude and the haunting shift of chords and aching melody in the E-Minor Prelude are among the many gems; the D-flat Major Prelude, nicknamed *Raindrop* because of a persistently repeated note, is similar in style to a Chopin nocturne and suggests a study in sustained melancholy. The A-Minor Prelude, written decades before anyone else would dare to thwart convention, finds Chopin shifting harmonies unsteadily and offering no clear-cut melodic line; it is difficult to know where the music is going, yet the ear holds on, riveted to the possibilities.

The Unanswered Question, Charles Ives (1908): Always ahead of his time, Ives conceived of music in ways that other composers wouldn't try for several more decades. In construction and content, this piece remains one of the twentieth century's most original. The question being considered is existence: Why are we here? Or, perhaps, how are we here? Or, are we alone? The questioner is a solo trumpet, with a pleading, unsettled phrase repeated, almost identically, several times. A quartet of flutes (sometimes placed in a balcony during performance) attempts to answer, but each answer gets increasingly dissonant, agitated, and inconclusive. While this is going on, and after all the questions and responses have been uttered, the strings calmly play a series of tonal chord progressions that form an otherworldly hymn, suggesting the eternity of the universe. *The Unanswered Question* can also be savored as pure abstraction. Either way, it's a work guaranteed to get you thinking. And wondering.

Variations for Orchestra, op. 31, Arnold Schoenberg (1926): The revolutionary, dissonant style known as twelve-tone (or serial) music has frightened many listeners since it was first proposed and demonstrated by Schoenberg in the early 1920s. But with patient listening, the expressiveness of atonality can become apparent. Consider the *Variations for Orchestra.* The score opens with a slow, vapory introduction, full of delicate hints at what is to come (and one obvious hint—a trombone intones four notes that, in German musical notation, spell out the name B-A-C-H). Then comes the theme, an angular, but somehow lyrical, melody. Nine variations follow, offering a startling array of orchestral shades, complex rhythms, and varying moods in the process. Toward the end, the B-A-C-H theme reappears to add a kind of dramatic counterpoint to Schoenberg's theme. The imposing logic and scope of the score places it high among works of twentieth-century abstract art. Although this work is not easy to digest, even after several hearings, it can handsomely repay the effort.

Violin Concerto, Alban Berg (1935): Notable music is occasionally born because of death. This concerto is one of the most sublime examples. Berg was very fond of Manon Gropius, the charming daughter of Alma Mahler (widow of composer Gustav Mahler) and architect Walter Gropius. When Manon died of polio at eighteen in 1935, Berg decided to commemorate her in a concerto that he dedicated "To the Memory of an Angel." The result was a twentieth-century classic.

Although Berg was a disciple of Schoenberg and the twelve-tone style, he decided to fuse that atonal method with traditional tonality. The two styles coexist in a way that brings added weight to both. Organizationally, the score is a model of symmetry. There are two movements, each with two parts. The tempos of each part produce a mirror effect in the concerto: slow-fast-fast-slow. Into the melodic material derived from the violin's haunting initial theme, Berg incorporates an Austrian folk song that had significance in his life and, most poetically, the tune from a chorale by Bach—"Es ist genug!" ("It is enough!"), which conveys a calm acceptance of death. The music for both violin and orchestra in the concerto is highly intricate, sometimes violent. But when, in the final section, Berg introduces that gentle reference to Bach, the work takes on a calming spirituality that can affect even the most unsuspecting or resistant listener.

Violin Concerto in D Major, op. 61, Ludwig van Beethoven (1806): Beethoven penned some of his finest music, including several sonatas, for violin. With his Violin Concerto, he not only produced a work of surpassing eloquence, but also provided an indelible model that would serve composers for several generations. He achieved an ideal balance between the instrumental forces, setting up a tightly woven dialogue rather than a case of violin versus orchestra. While there are plenty of opportunities for the soloist to shine, the bravura element takes second place to the sensitive reflection.

A long, noble first movement, begun with soft, expectant beats of the timpani, is followed by a sublime slow movement. After so much seriousness, Beethoven lightens the mood with a delectable rondo. Like several of Beethoven's efforts, this concerto seems to straddle the fence between eighteenth-century Classicism and nineteenth-century Romanticism.

Violin Concerto in D Minor, op. 47, Jean Sibelius (1904): This concerto demonstrates how Sibelius, the organic farmer of music, approached composition. He planted his melodic ideas deep in the purest soil. When they first emerge, these themes can sound fragmentary and diffuse, but Sibelius invariably harvests them— cross-pollinates them, you might say—in such a way that they develop into a clear, firm statement. They grow, well, organically.

The concerto's first movement, enshrouded in mist at the beginning, contains seemingly unrelated ideas that gradually take shape in gripping fashion. The violin is more of an extension of the orchestra than a show-offy solo instrument; for that matter, the orchestra becomes an extension of the violin at times. This fusion, and the prevailing earthiness of the music (especially the propulsive finale), make this one of the most distinctive and arresting of all violin concertos.

War Requiem, Benjamin Britten (1962): Britten was a confirmed pacifist who claimed conscientious objector status in World War II. He found an ideal musical outlet for his strong beliefs when he was commissioned to write a work for the 1962 dedication of the new Coventry Cathedral in England, built literally in the shadow of the bombed-out ruins of the original church, destroyed by German bombs in 1940.

Britten started with the ancient Latin text of the Catholic Mass for the Dead to form a memorial to the victims of all wars. Into this text he wove haunting poems by antiwar poet Wilfred Owen, who was killed in action a week before the armistice that ended World War I. Adding to the impact of the words was Britten's original, symbolic choice of soloists—a British tenor, a German baritone, and a Russian soprano—representing three countries particularly devastated by the Second World War.

The *War Requiem* is on a vast scale, written for full orchestra, a separate chamber orchestra (to accompany the tenor and baritone solos), a large chorus, a boys' choir, and an organ. But the highly personal nature of the words and music gives the piece an intimate, involving quality. Britten's style makes distinctive use of dissonance, as well as tonality, to produce a soundscape unlike anyone else's. The work achieves true profundity, from the horrific imagery of the *Dies Irae* ("Day of Judgment"), when hell is equated with the brutality of war, to the touching finale, when two soldiers from opposite armies confront each other after death and find common ground in sleep. The twentieth century, which was so often disturbed by war, found in this work a fitting, disturbing, and ultimately cleansing response.

EIGHT

Classical Music on CD

In addition to frequent concertgoing, the best way for the Curious Listener to expand knowledge and appreciation of classical music is by building a basic library of recordings.

This is not necessarily the greatest time to be assembling such a library, however. Since the 1990s, major record companies have significantly reduced their traditionally modest commitment to the classical market; there are fewer and fewer new releases in stores these days, fewer recordings documenting the music makers of our time.

The flip side of this development has a silver lining—many truly classic classical recordings from the past continue to be remastered with better sound and repackaged in a variety of ways, almost always at a budget price. Also, with the big companies recording less, several smaller labels have entered the picture in recent years, making many highly credible performances available, again usually at low retail cost. So with careful shopping, it's definitely possible to acquire a solid collection of recordings, practically for a song.

Individual tastes will, in the long run, determine the extent and characteristics of a compact disc library. But it's well worth starting out with a broad and balanced view of the repertoire, providing a solid foundation that can be built upon indefinitely.

Ultimately, a CD collection should include recordings of everything in the previous chapter, but the following list represents a mixture of those towering works and other notable, popular pieces. This suggested core of recordings, chosen for both the music itself and the caliber of the performances, should help satisfy and engage curious ears—and whet the aural appetite for more.

You'll notice several decades-old, predigital (even prestereo) recordings among the items, by the way. They have been included because the quality of the music making is so strong, and, besides, the recorded sound is never less than adequate. Listening to both today's and yesterday's classical artists is also a good way to expand appreciation of an absolutely essential ingredient in music—interpretation.

Because compact discs are constantly going out of print (sometimes to be reincarnated later), most of these sixty recommended items are those that already have proven staying power in the catalogues, so they should be available for some time to come. And many of the choices here are easy on the budget, making a basic collection all the more practical.

Adagio for Strings and Violin Concerto, Samuel Barber; Isaac Stern, violinist; New York Philharmonic; Leonard Bernstein, conductor (Sony Classical): The *Adagio for Strings*, long one of the most beloved items in the American repertoire (given additional popularity thanks to the film *Platoon*), invariably pulls the listener in with its elegiac mood and deep poignancy. Bernstein conducts a loving performance with the New York Philharmonic on a disc that also includes Barber's rapturous Violin Concerto.

Appalachian Spring **Suite,** *Fanfare for the Common Man, Billy the Kid* **Suite, Four Dance Episodes from** *Rodeo,* **Aaron Copland; New York Philharmonic; Leonard Bernstein, conductor (Sony Classical):** Bernstein and Copland were not just friends, but musical soul mates, so when Bernstein conducted Copland, the results invariably sizzled. These performances of ever-popular works have long been treasured for their rhythmic vitality and sensitivity to the composer's unique idiom.

Bolero, Daphnis et Chloe **Suite no. 2,** *La Valse,* **et al., Maurice Ravel; Montreal Symphony Orchestra; Charles Dutoit, conductor (London):** Dutoit's affinity for Ravel was forever established with his recording of the complete *Daphnis et Chloe* ballet score in the early 1980s, which remains highly recommended (also on the London label). The tight rapport between the conductor and his superb Montreal ensemble is no less persuasive in their sensual, virtuosic recording of the Suite no. 2 from that ballet on a disc that includes other Ravel favorites that belong in any classical collection, among them *Bolero* and *La Valse*. There's also a specially priced, two-disc Ravel set with Dutoit and the Montreal Symphony that contains these performances and adds still more of the composer's output.

Brandenburg **Concertos, Johann Sebastian Bach; Amsterdam Baroque Orchestra; Ton Koopman, conductor (Erato):** The six, consistently engaging *Brandenburg* Concertos (dedicated to the Margrave of Brandenburg, who apparently never even looked at them) truly come to life on original instruments of the Baroque era. Koopman and his ensemble bring out a wealth of details in these rhythmically crisp, historically informed performances.

Candide Overture, Symphonic Dances from *West Side Story, On the Waterfront* Symphonic Suite, *Fancy Free,* Leonard Bernstein; New York Philharmonic, Bernstein, conductor (Sony Classical): If Bernstein had written nothing but the effervescent *Candide* Overture, he would still be celebrated; that work gets a crackling performance here by the composer's longtime orchestra. The alternately bracing and tender Symphonic Dances from Bernstein's Broadway hit *West Side Story* and other pieces receive equally memorable accounts.

Carmina Burana, Carl Orff; Thomas Allen, baritone; Sheila Armstrong, soprano; Gerald English, tenor; London Symphony Orchestra and Chorus; Andre Previn, conductor (EMI Classics): This "secular cantata," with its earthy Medieval texts, hypnotic rhythms, and often splashy orchestral effects, is one of the most familiar works in the repertoire, used frequently in films and commercials. It is hardly a profound piece, but it sounds wonderfully inspired in this performance led with a sure hand by Previn, who gets consistently dynamic singing and playing from his forces.

Cello Concerto in B Minor, op. 104, Antonín Dvořák; Mstislav Rostropovich, cellist; Berlin Philharmonic; Herbert von Karajan, conductor (Deutsche Grammophon): This concerto, with its combination of drama and intense lyricism, has received several outstanding performances on disc. Among the most exalted is this one from the 1960's. Rostropovich is to this music born; he gets to the heart and soul of the piece. And Karajan is a masterful partner, coaxing superb playing from the Philharmonic.

Clarinet Quintet in B Minor, op. 115, Johannes Brahms; Richard Stoltzman, clarinetist; the Tokyo String Quartet (RCA Red Seal): For pure beauty of form and content, few chamber-music works offer more than this quintet for clarinet and strings. And for pure beauty of tone and expression, few clarinetists can match Stoltzman, whose recording with the refined Tokyo ensemble remains a gem.

Concerto for Orchestra, **Béla Bártok; Chicago Symphony Orchestra; Fritz Reiner, conductor (RCA Living Stereo):** In this vintage recording from the 1950s, the Chicago Symphony takes full advantage of the opportunities to show off its mettle in Bártok's dazzling showpiece under the intuitive guidance of Fritz Reiner. The performance has never lost its status among collectors.

Dichterliebe, **Robert Schumann; Ian Bostridge, tenor; Julius Drake, pianist (EMI Classics):** This song cycle of longing, love, and loss is tailormade for the innately expressive tone and thoughtful styling of Bostridge, whose performance with pianist Julius Drake is one of the best lieder recordings in years. If you're sure you could never like lieder or a classical tenor, give this a listen. You just may get hooked on both.

Die schone Mullerin, **Franz Schubert; Dietrich Fischer-Dieskau, baritone; Gerald Moore, pianist (EMI Classics):** There has probably been no more incisive or vocally beautiful interpreter of Schubert lieder than Fischer-Dieskau. He made more than one exemplary re-cording of the song cycle *Die schone Mullerin* ("The Fair Maid of the Mill"); this one, his second, with peerless accompanist Gerald Moore, has understandably been rereleased on EMI's series called "Great Recordings of the Century."

11,000 *Virgins: Chants for the Feast of St. Ursula,* Hildegard of Bingen; Anonymous 4 (Harmonia Mundi): Here's a terrific sampling of some of the oldest extant music, by one of music history's most fas-cinating figures. These chants from nearly a millennium ago, celebrating St. Ursula (said to have been martyred with eleven thousand virgins—hence the disc's catchy title), are sung with remarkable purity of tone and sensitivity to style by the female quartet Anonymous 4.

***Enigma* Variations, op. 36, *Falstaff,* op. 68, Edward Elgar; Philharmonia Orchestra; Sir John Barbirolli, conductor (EMI Classics):** The ingenuity and potency of the *Enigma Variations* the first great symphonic masterpiece of British music, brings out the best in Barbirolli, who had a knack for getting deep into Elgar's sound-world. His is one of the most satisfying accounts of the *Enigma* Variations. And the companion selection, the colorful tone poem *Falstaff,* gets a winning performance, too.

***Firebird* Suite, *The Rite of Spring,* and *Persephone,* Igor Stravinsky; San Francisco Symphony Orchestra; Michael Tilson Thomas, conductor (RCA Red Seal):** Tilson Thomas reveals a disarming mastery of the Stravinsky idiom in his accounts of two essential Stravinsky scores, *Firebird* and *The Rite of Spring,* as well as the lesser known *Persephone.* The San Franciscans offer abundant rhythmic crispness and earthy vitality in the *Rite*; the shimmering beauty of *Firebird* comes through especially well.

Four Last Songs, et al., Richard Strauss; Jessye Norman, soprano; Gewandhaus Orchestra; Kurt Masur, conductor (Philips): Strauss's own swan songs—four lieder with texts by Hermann Hesse and Josef von Eichendorf about approaching death—requires great sensitivity as well as technical control from a singer. Jessye Norman, recorded in her prime, gives a sumptuous performance in long, long breaths that allow the music to float on eloquent wings of song; Masur provides supple, eloquent support. Several other Strauss lieder fill out this golden recording.

The Four Seasons, Antonio Vivaldi; Giuliano Carmignola, violinist; Venice Baroque Orchestra; Andrea Marcon, conductor (Sony Classical): This Baroque favorite has attracted many of the world's leading violinists, so there are lots of high-profile recordings available. But this music doesn't call so much for a star soloist as it does for a cohesive, perfectly balanced effort between soloist and ensemble. And you'd have a hard time finding a better example than on this period-instrument disc, which delivers incredible virtuosity, dynamic coloring, and visceral phrasing.

Goldberg Variations, Johann Sebastian Bach; Glenn Gould, pianist (Sony Classical): When Gould recorded this keyboard masterpiece in 1955, he shook up the music world. This interpretation has a power, individuality, depth, and sheer genius that still astonishes decades later. Note that there is more than one Gould performance of the *Goldberg* Variations; all have their merits, the 1955 classic is the one to get.

Great Pianists of the Century, Arthur Rubinstein (Philips): Every classical CD collection has to include a sampling of Chopin's solo piano music—and of Arthur Rubinstein playing it. A superb collection of nocturnes, polonaises, mazurkas, waltzes, and more is contained on this two-disc set, which exemplifies the genius of Chopin and Rubinstein in equal measure.

Mass in B Minor, Johann Sebastian Bach; Monteverdi Choir, English Baroque Soloists; John Eliot Gardiner (Deutsche Grammophon): This monument to Bach's genius has done well on recordings, but pride of place goes to Gardiner's performance with his top-notch vocal and instrumental forces. It achieves an effective balance between purely historical considerations—original instruments and their transparent textures, tempos that have the authentic dancelike momentum of the Baroque era—and interpretive expression. This is not a history lesson, but a deeply felt, involving account of Bach's testament of music and faith.

***Messiah,* Handel; Monteverdi Choir, English Baroque Soloists; John Eliot Gardiner (Philips):** Once again, you can't go wrong with Gardiner and these superbly matched ensembles. The recording reflects what is best about the effort to re-create authentic performance practice, offering lively tempos, transparent textures, and tasteful ornamentation of solo vocal lines. This popular oratorio, which used to be routinely performed in a thick manner left over from the days of Victorian piety, reveals its brilliant construction, as well as genuine religious sentiment, in this stylistically informed, always expressive performance.

***Missa Papae Marcelli,* Giovanni Palestrina; *Miserere,* Gregorio Allegri; Westminster Abbey Choir; Simon Preston, conductor (Deutsche Grammo-**

phon Archiv): Palestrina's magnum opus receives a richly sung account from a top-drawer chorus and a conductor with a keen appreciation for the inner workings of the score. It's a striking demonstration of the musical glory of the Renaissance.

Orchestral Works, Vol. 1, Claude Debussy; ORTF Orchestra; Jean Martinon, conductor (EMI Classics): This budget-priced, two-disc set includes several of Debussy's greatest orchestral scores, including *La Mer* and *Prelude to the Afternoon of a Faun*. The conductor and orchestra have impeccable French credentials, bringing to the music considerable subtlety, refinement, and poetic sensibility. For another splendid account of *La Mer*, consider the one by Charles Munch and the Boston Symphony Orchestra (RCA Living Stereo), which has the distinct advantage of also containing the classic, knockout performance from 1959 of another French masterwork, Camille Saint-Saens's Symphony no. 3 (*Organ*).

Piano Concerto in G, Maurice Ravel; Piano Concerto no. 3 in C, op. 26, Sergei Prokofiev; Martha Argerich, pianist; Berlin Philharmonic; Claudio Abbado, conductor (Deutsche Grammophon): These two colorful, exhilarating, and sensual concertos are tailor-made for the superhuman technique and expressive powers of Argerich, whose collaboration with Abbado and the Berlin Philharmonic retains almost legendary status. The pianist revels in Ravel's jazzy touches in the outer movements and captures the essence of the haunting reverie in between, letting it float unhurriedly, as if in a dream. The Prokofiev concerto's underlying kinetic power and bursts of incandescent lyricism inspire an arresting performance. Filling out the disc is a powerhouse account of Ravel's solo piano piece *Gaspard de la nuit*.

Piano Concerto no. 1 in B-flat Minor, op. 23, Peter Ilyich Tchaikovsky, Piano Concerto no. 2 in C Minor, op. 18, Sergei Rachmaninoff; Van Cliburn, pianist; RCA Symphony Orchestra; Kiril Kondrashin, conductor; Chicago Symphony Orchestra; Fritz Reiner, conductor (RCA Red Seal): Shortly after his historic win at the Tchaikovsky Competition in Moscow in 1958, Cliburn recorded these concertos, two of the most popular works in all of classical music. His technical virtuosity remains stunning to hear, as does his ability to infuse the familiar scores with a combination of poetic expression and Romantic grandeur. He enjoys tight support from Kondrashin in the Tchaikovsky warhorse, Reiner in the Rachmaninoff.

Piano Concerto no. 2 in B-flat Major, op. 83, *Variations on a Theme of Haydn,* op. 56a, Johannes Brahms; Horacio Gutierrez, pianist; Royal Philharmonic Orchestra; Andre Previn, conductor (Telarc): The journey from dramatic tension to playfulness in this concerto calls for a soloist with both technical prowess and natural poetic instincts. Gutierrez provides that combination in a fresh performance ably backed by Previn and the Royal Philharmonic. But note that a much older recording still commands attention, the one featuring pianist Leon Fleisher with George Szell leading the Cleveland Orchestra (Sony Classical) on a low-priced, two-disc set that also offers the Piano Concerto no. 1 in D Minor.

Piano Concerto no. 5 in E-flat Major, op. 73 (*Emperor*), and no. 2 in B-flat Major, op. 19, Ludwig van Beethoven; Evgeny Kissin, pianist; Philharmonia Orchestra; James Levine, conductor (Sony Classical): The *Emperor* Concerto's symphonic scale and heroic writing for the piano provide great challenges that have been handsomely met by many eminent soloists over the decades. The performance by Kissin, the Russian keyboard dynamo, holds its own against the competition, offering in equal measures bravura and sensitivity. He receives stylish backing from Levine and the Philharmonia.

Piano Concerto no. 20 in D Minor, K. 466, Piano Concerto no. 27 in B-flat Major, K. 595, Wolfgang Amadeus Mozart; Murray Perahia, pianist and conductor; English Chamber Orchestra (Sony Classical): As always with Mozart, it's impossible to settle on just a couple of his works in any genre, let alone the twenty-seven piano concertos. But these two examples provide a compelling sense of the expressive range he could achieve with the combination of keyboard and orchestra, and the performances by Perahia with the English Chamber Orchestra are among the most refined, personal, and deeply satisfying ever committed to disc.

Piano Quintet in A Major *(Trout),* Franz Schubert; Pamela Frank, violinist; Rebecca Young, violist; Yo-Yo Ma, cellist; Edgar Meyer, bassist; Emanuel Ax, pianist (Sony Classical): Overflowing as it does with tunefulness, charm, and imagination, the *Trout* Quintet tends to bring out the best in players, which it does here. It's not just a matter of tight cohesiveness, but of a fresh spirit, a contagious enthusiasm for each turn of phrase.

Piano Quintet in E-flat Major, op. 44, Piano Quartet in E-flat Major, op. 47, Robert Schumann; Menahem Pressler, pianist; Emerson String Quartet (Deutsche Grammophon): These two pieces represent Schumann's finest contributions to the chamber-music repertoire, while the slow movement of the Piano Quartet represents all by itself the very soul of Romanticism. Pressler and the Emerson ensemble reveal full appreciation of the poetic riches in both scores, occupying the same, tight wavelength.

Piano Sonatas no. 8 in C Minor, op. 13 *(Pathetique),* **no. 14 in C-sharp Minor, op. 27, no. 27, no. 2** *(Moonlight),* **no. 21 in C Major, op. 53** *(Waldstein),* **and no. 23 in F Minor, op. 57** *(Appassionata),* **Ludwig van Beethoven; Wilhelm Kempff, pianist (Deutsche Grammophon):** An ideal introduction to Beethoven's piano sonatas is contained on this single disc. From the famous, moody opening of the *Moonlight* Sonata and dark drama of the *Pathetique* to the almost giddy force of the *Waldstein* and unbridled emotions of the *Appassionata,* Kempff puts his patrician stamp on the music.

Requiem, Giuseppe Verdi; Elisabeth Schwarzkopf, soprano; Crista Ludwig, mezzo-soprano; Nicolai Gedda, tenor; Nicolai Ghiaurov, bass; Philharmonia Orchestra and Chorus; Carlo Maria Giulini, conductor (EMI Classics): This shattering work, with its reflection on the horrors of death and the uncertainties of what comes after, inspires a virtually definitive performance on this 1960s recording. Giulini's rich insight into the score unleashes both the shattering impact of the *Dies Irae*'s fire and brimstone and the full tenderness of the score's lyrical passages. His efforts are complemented by stellar singing from the soloists and chorus, vibrant playing from the Philharmonia.

Rhapsody in Blue, An American in Paris, **George Gershwin;** *Grand Canyon Suite,* **Ferde Grofe; Columbia Symphony Orchestra and New York Philharmonic; Leonard Bernstein, pianist and conductor (Sony Classical):** The two Gershwin favorites, with their marvelously American confidence and charm, ignite sparks from Leonard Bernstein. His idiomatic, galvanizing 1959 performance of the *Rhapsody,* conducting the Columbia Symphony Orchestra from the keyboard, will never go out of style. He also brings out the full character of *An American in Paris* and the naive charm of the Grofe work with the New York Philharmonic.

Scheherezade, Nikolai Rimsky-Korsakov; Royal Philharmonic Orchestra; Sir Thomas Beecham, conductor (EMI Classics): Rimsky-Korsakov's evocation of tales from the *Thousand and One Nights* is all about orchestral coloring and aural entertainment, which makes it perfectly suited to Beecham's particular talents. In this golden-oldie recording from the 1950s, he extracts the work's delightful character in a vibrant performance from the Royal Philharmonic; another crowd pleaser, the *Polovtsian Dances* from Borodin's opera *Prince Igor*, fills out the disc.

String Quartet in F, op. 96 *(American)***, Antonín Dvořák; String Quartet no. 1 in D Major, op. 11, Peter Ilyich Tchaikovsky; String Quartet no. 2 in D Major, Alexander Borodin; Emerson String Quartet (Deutsche Grammophon):** The *American*, among Dvořák's most ingratiating chamber pieces and a great example of nineteenth-century Romanticism, gets a sterling performance by the Emerson String Quartet on a moderately priced collection that offers two more treasurable pieces from the same era by Tchaikovsky and Borodin (both of those works contain a movement that has long been on the classical hit parade, frequently played out of its original context—Tchaikovsky's *Andante cantabile* and Borodin's Nocturne).

String Quartet in G Minor, Claude Debussy; String Quartet in F Major, Maurice Ravel; Emerson String Quartet (Deutsche Grammophon): These two luminous works, which share much in common stylistically and atmospherically, call for the kind of technical refinement and sensitive phrasing that are hallmarks of the Emerson ensemble. The performances are sensual, involving, and revealing.

String Quartets, op. 76, nos. 2–4, Joseph Haydn; Alban Berg Quartet (EMI Classics): Haydn's mastery of the string quartet form reached a pinnacle in the six pieces of op. 76. The last three, including the beloved *Emperor* and *Sunrise* quartets, receive finely polished, aristocratic accounts from the Alban Berg Quartet.

***Also Sprach Zarathustra, Ein Heldenleben, Eine Alpensinfonie, Don Juan, Till Eulenspiegel,* Richard Strauss; Chicago Symphony Orchestra, Vienna Philharmonic, Bavarian Radio Symphony Orchestra; Georg Solti, conductor (London/Decca):** There's nothing quite like the experience of a first-rate conductor and orchestra charging into a symphonic poem by Strauss. You get one such conductor and three such orchestras in this budget-priced, double-disc collection, which offers five of the most colorful Strauss scores in vividly detailed performances.

***Symphonie fantastique,* Hector Berlioz; Orchestre Revolutionnaire et Romantique; John Eliot Gardiner, conductor (Philips):** Because this revolutionary, convention-shattering work paved the way for the full blossoming of Romantic music, it's fitting to hear a recording of the score by forces who are both revolutionary and romantic—Gardiner's top-notch ensemble of period instruments. Adding to the attraction of this release is the fact that it was recorded in the hall where *Symphonie fantastique* was first heard in 1830, and that the performance uses every instrument Berlioz called for, including six harps. There simply is no other account of the piece like it, and none more revelatory.

Symphonies nos. 1–9, Ludwig van Beethoven; Vienna Philharmonic; Leonard Bernstein, conductor (Deutsche Grammophon): Shopping for individual performances of these symphonies is part of the fun of building a record collection, but to get started, a complete set makes great sense (it's usually more economical, too). Choosing a set is very complicated, though. Nowadays, you have your pick not only of complete Beethoven symphony cycles conducted by history's most gifted conductors and played by the world's greatest orchestras, but several more cycles performed on instruments of Beethoven's day, an option previous generations of record buyers could not have imagined. As an initial investment, opting for a modern-day orchestra is perhaps the best; it's how you will hear the symphonies most often performed in concerts. For intensely personal interpretations of the Beethoven nine, the choice is clearly Bernstein and the Vienna Philharmonic; they enjoyed uncanny rapport that produced electric results whenever they collaborated on German repertoire. This is a vital, involving achievement. For a traditional outlook, you can't go wrong with the comfortably priced set with George Szell conducting the Cleveland Orchestra (Sony Classical). For Beethoven in historically authentic style, no version offers more conviction and imagination than that by the Orchestre Revolutionnaire et Romantique, conducted by John Eliot Gardiner (Deutsche Grammophon Archiv). There is also a very convincing compromise choice, which nearly offers the best of both worlds, historic and modern—the Chamber Orchestra of Europe, conducted by Nikolaus Harnoncourt (Teldec).

Symphonies nos. 1–4, Johannes Brahms; Cleveland Orchestra; George Szell, conductor (Sony Classical): Every classical collection should include all four of the Brahms symphonies, with their striking combination of poetry and power. As is the case with Beethoven's nine, you can certainly choose individual discs, getting a variety of conductors and orchestras in the process. But there's nothing wrong with settling on one complete set to start, especially when it has the bonus of a budget price. George Szell, who had an intuitive understanding of Brahms, generates thoroughly accomplished, ever-expressive performances with the Clevelanders. For something completely different, you might want to consider Leonard Bernstein's recordings with the Vienna Philharmonic (Deutsche Grammophon). The conductor's intense molding and rhythmic stretching of the scores may not be everyone's idea of how to approach Brahms, but the imagination and emotional depth involved make a potent statement.

Symphony no. 1 and *Of Rage and Remembrance,* John Corigliano; Michelle de Young, mezzo-soprano; Washington Oratorio Society, Washington Choral Arts Society, National Symphony Orchestra; Leonard Slatkin, conductor (RCA Red Seal): The shattering reaction to the toll of AIDS encompassed in Symphony no. 1 is not easy listening, but Slatkin makes it imperative listening. He gets deep into the heart of this angry, confrontational, ultimately touching score and summons playing of searing power. Corigliano's choral work, *Of Rage and Remembrance*, uses music from the third movement of the symphony, putting into words what the other score expresses in sound alone. It makes a powerful addition to the disc.

Symphony no. 1 in D Major, Gustav Mahler; Florida Philharmonic; James Judd, conductor (Harmonia Mundi): The mix of mystery, irony, folk-like melody, and sheer exuberance makes the First Symphony an ideal introduction to Mahler's sound-world. There are more renowned performances of the work, but Judd's idiomatic con-

ducting and the sensitive response from the Florida Philharmonic give this version an irresistible pull. There is, above all,
a sense of spontaneity here, as well as remarkable rhythmic
freedom (especially in the second movement). An added bonus
is a lovely account of the *Blumine* movement, which Mahler
eliminated from his final version of this symphony. On top of
everything else, the disc has been rereleased at a bargain price.

**Symphony no. 2, *The Unanswered Question, Central Park in the Dark,* et.
al., Charles Ives; New York Philharmonic; Leonard Bernstein, conductor
(Deutsche Grammophon):** America's most original composer found
an ideal interpreter in Bernstein, who seemed to thrive on
Ives's quirky melodic material and often audacious ideas about
orchestration and musical structure. The conductor, who gave
the belated premiere of Ives's Second Symphony, brings out the
score's humor and vigorous spirit here. He also captures the
mystery and dark beauty of *The Unanswered Question.* The disc
contains several other Ives gems, all performed with flair by
the New York Philharmonic.

**Symphony no. 2 in D Major, op. 43, and no. 6 in D Minor, op. 104, Jean
Sibelius; London Symphony Orchestra; Sir Colin Davis, conductor (RCA Red
Seal):** Davis, one of the most insightful interpreters of Sibelius
on disc, offers a typically telling, arresting account of the composer's mighty Second Symphony. The London Symphony contributes playing consistently rich in technical brilliance and
expressive intensity. There's an equally impressive performance
of the less familiar Symphony no. 6. For just about the same
price, however, you might consider a larger dose of Sibelius,
featuring stellar conductors and orchestras, including Symphony
no. 1, conducted by Leopold Stokowski; Symphony no. 2, con-

ducted by Thomas Schippers; and the Violin Concerto, with violinist Zino Francescatti and conductor Leonard Bernstein. It's all on a two-disc, budget set from Sony Classical.

Symphony no. 3 in A Minor, op. 56 *(Scottish),* **and no. 4 in A Major, op. 90** *(Italian),* **Felix Mendelssohn; London Symphony Orchestra; Claudio Abbado, conductor (Deutsche Grammophon):** Abbado relishes Mendelssohn's unending supply of great tunes and his inventive way of using them in these two symphonic postcards. The conductor coaxes a keen appreciation for subtlety, as well as color and vitality, from the orchestra.

Symphony no. 4 in F Minor, op. 36, no. 5 in E Minor, op. 64, and no. 6 in B Minor *(Pathetique),* **Peter Ilyich Tchaikovsky; Leningrad Philharmonic; Evgeny Mravinsky, conductor (Deutsche Grammophon):** The last three of Tchaikovsky's numbered symphonies have long been among his most popular works, offering tremendous drama and outpourings of indelible melody. Back in 1960, Evgeny Mravinsky recorded this trio of hits with the Leningrad Philharmonic and the results remain in a special class. These thoroughly idiomatic, very Russian performances take full advantage of every dramatic outburst in the scores, every heart-tugging moment of melancholy or longing. And the playing is top-notch throughout, nowhere more so than in the incredible whirl of the Fourth Symphony's finale.

Symphony No. 5 in C-sharp Minor, Gustav Mahler; Vienna Philharmonic; Leonard Bernstein, conductor (Deutsche Grammophon): The combination of Mahler and Bernstein ignited some of the twentieth century's most memorable, uplifting performances. The conductor responded with particular intensity and insight to the darkness-into-light outline of the Fifth Symphony, lingering to exquisite effect over the famous "Adagietto" movement. The Vienna Philharmonic, as usual, gives Bernstein everything he asks for and more.

Symphony No. 5 in D Minor, op. 47; Dmitri Shostakovich; National Symphony Orchestra; Mstislav Rostropovich, conductor (Teldec): Few conductors have as deeply personal a connection to this work as Rostropovich. His interpretation, splendidly played by the National Symphony, is unlike anyone else's. Tempos, whether fast or slow, can be extreme; phrases can take unexpected turns or receive unusual jolts. But the visceral emotion behind the performance is simply stunning. Rostropovich considers the final moments of the score to be a musical metaphor for the screams of Stalin's victims, and conducts it accordingly. It's an unforgettable effect.

Symphony no. 8 in B Minor *(Unfinished)* and no. 9 in C Major *(The Great)*, Franz Schubert; Staatskapelle Dresden; Giuseppe Sinopoli, conductor: The late Sinopoli, who earned a degree in psychiatry, had a way of burrowing deep into a score and finding out what made it tick. His analayses of these Schubert works, especially the *Unfinished*, are never pedantic, but full of beautiful detail and deeply considered ideas. The Staatskapelle Dresden turns in polished, warmhearted playing.

Symphony no. 8 in G Major, op. 88, and no. 9 in E Minor, op. 95 *(From the New World)*, Antonín Dvořák; Berlin Philharmonic; Rafael Kubelik, conductor (Deutsche Grammophon): In these sterling performances from the 1970s, Kubelik and the Berlin Philharmonic convey the Czech spirit, sensitive nuances, and lyrical drive of both symphonies. Also well worth keeping an eye out for are the recordings from a decade earlier with Istvan Kertesz conducting the London Symphony Orchestra; they are unrivaled.

Symphony no. 40 in G Minor, K. 550, and no. 41 in C Major, K. 551 (*Jupiter*), Wolfgang Amadeus Mozart; Prague Chamber Orchestra; Sir Charles Mackerras, conductor (Telarc): From the haunting shades of melancholy in no. 40 to the nobility of spirit in no. 41, these final works by Mozart in the symphonic form are crowning examples of his genius. They have both been amply and ably recorded, which makes it tough selecting one. Mackerras is to the Mozart manner born, and he leads finely etched, rhythmically propulsive accounts with the Prague ensemble.

Symphony no. 101 in D Major (*The Clock*) and no. 104 in D Major (*London*), Joseph Haydn; Orchestra of St. Luke's; Sir Charles Mackerras, conductor (Telarc): To get a taste of how Haydn earned the title "Father of the Symphony," these two items from the last twelve symphonies he wrote provide much to savor. The inventiveness and wit of no. 101 (nicknamed *The Clock* for reasons you'll hear in the second movement) and no. 104 come through at every turn in these crisp, elegant performances by Mackerras and the St. Luke's ensemble.

Violin Concerto, John Adams; Violin Concerto, Philip Glass; Robert McDuffie, violinist; Houston Symphony Orchestra; Christoph Eschenbach, conductor (Telarc): The musical style of minimalism has produced few works as compelling and simply beautiful as these two concertos. The hypnotic Glass score adds richly lyrical ideas above simple harmonies and repetitive patterns, especially in the second movement; the Adams concerto, more complex in style, more dramatic in character, is equally arresting. Robert McDuffie proves ideal in both pieces, using his shining technical skills and intuitive phrasing to tap the strengths of both scores. The Houston Symphony Orchestra, conducted by Christoph Eschenbach, is also very much in the minimalist groove.

Violin Concerto, Alban Berg; Violin Concerto in D Major, Igor Stravinsky; Itzhak Perlman, violinist; Seiji Ozawa, conductor (Deutsche Grammophon): There is no better evidence of how beautiful and heartfelt music in an atonal style can be than Berg's concerto, especially when played with such angelic warmth and technical aplomb as it is here by Perlman. He likewise soars through the Stravinsky concerto, enjoying smooth support from Ozawa and the Bostonians.

Violin Concerto in D Major, op. 61, Ludwig van Beethoven; Violin Concerto in E Minor, op. 64, Felix Mendelssohn; Yehudi Menuhin, violinist; Wilhelm Furtwängler, conductor (EMI Classics): The noble Beethoven concerto has yielded a large number of noble performances on disc, but top honors still go to this venerable 1953 recording featuring two of the most inspired and inspiring musicians of the twentieth century. Menuhin penetrates to the heart of the score with second-nature partnering from Furtwängler; their efforts are simply transcendent, as rich in poetry as in power. The two men produce no less revelatory results in the endearing Mendelssohn concerto.

Violin Concerto in D Major, op. 35, Peter Ilyich Tchaikovsky; Violin Concerto in D Major, op. 77, Johannes Brahms; Jascha Heifetz, violinist; Chicago Symphony Orchestra; Fritz Reiner, conductor (RCA Red Seal): These two scores, which find their respective composers at their most ardent, could not be more suited to the legendary virtuosity of Jascha Heifetz. Others may bring more personal touches to parts of the concertos, but the overall Heifetz magic—supreme virtuosity and heartfelt phrasing—remains impossible to beat. Add in the equally revered Fritz Reiner leading the Chicago Symphony and the disc recommends itself.

Violin Sonata no. 1 in G Major, op. 78, no. 2 in A Major, op. 100, and no. 3 in D Minor, op. 108, Johannes Brahms; Aaron Rosand, violinist; Hugh Sung, pianist (Vox Classics): The combination of intense lyricism, intimate reflection, and bold relief of these sonatas finds an ideal interpreter in Rosand, one of the most eloquent and patrician, if underrated, violinists snce Heifetz. Sung is an attentive, if somewhat distantly recorded, partner.

The Wagner Collection; Vienna Philharmonic; Sir Georg Solti, conductor (London/Decca): Some Curious Listeners may not be curious enough to delve into Wagner operas, but an awareness and appreciation of the instrumental music from those operas is painless and essential. Wagner's revolutionary influence on the whole history of classical music can be heard in this broad collection of orchestral excerpts from *Tristan und Isolde, Tannhauser, The Flying Dutchman*, and more. Solti's command of the Wagnerian idiom is never in doubt, and he has one of the world's supreme Wagnerian exponents in the Vienna Philharmonic.

Water Music, George Frideric Handel; English Baroque Soloists; John Eliot Gardiner, conductor (Philips): Gardiner proves to be a convincing guide to recreating not just the sound, but the sense of occasion, that Handel achieved with his *Water Music*, which was first performed on a barge floating magisterially down the Thames. The playing by the English Baroque Soloists is full of startling colors and propelled by a contagious rhythmic flow.

Weekend in Vienna: Strauss Favorites; Vienna Philharmonic; Willi Boskovsky, conductor (London/Decca): The music of the Strauss family—lighthearted, but hardly light in value—releases its full power when played in authentic Viennese style, which almost always means by Viennese musicians. One of the most winsome interpreters of this repertoire was Boskovsky, who guides the Vienna Philharmonic through authentic and delectable performances of such favorites as *The Blue Danube*, the *Emperor Waltzes*, and *Pizzicato Polka*.

NINE

The Language of Classical Music

Like any specialized field, classical music has its own language, filled with terms that can seem alien to the uninitiated, but learning to "speak" this language is not really very difficult. Some of the most common musical terms used in this book are defined here, along with a few other words you are bound to come across while attending concerts or reading the liner notes of recordings.

This basic, beginning vocabulary of the art form should help the Curious Listener become more comfortable with venturing into the vast, inviting world of classical music.

A CAPPELLA: Choral music sung without instrumental accompaniment.

ACCELERANDO: A direction to increase the tempo.

ACCOMPANIMENT: The background, played by an instrument or instruments, to music for a solo instrument or voice.

ADAGIO: A slow tempo.

ALLEGRO: A fast tempo.

ALLEMANDE: A dance form, said to be of German origin, usually placed first in suites of Baroque instrumental music and played fairly fast.

ANDANTE: A moderate tempo. The term, which comes from the Italian for "to walk," suggests a normal walking speed.

ARIA: A composition for solo voice, typically found in a cantata, oratorio, Mass, Requiem, and other nontheatrical works, as well as opera.

ART SONG: A general term to describe a composition for voice and piano (or other instruments) with a text usually drawn from poetry and having a written-out accompaniment.

ATONALITY: A musical style developed in the early twentieth century that eliminates previously accepted rules of harmony, creating a dissonant language of expression.

BASSO CONTINUO: A type of instrumental accompaniment in Baroque music, usually for harpsichord, that involves a bass line and indications of what chords should be played above that line.

BATON: A thin stick used by a conductor, primarily to indicate rhythm.

CADENZA: A passage near the end of a movement in a concerto when the solo instrument plays without accompaniment from the orchestra and explores in a free-form style melodic material from that movement.

CANON: A musical form of follow-the-leader in which a single melodic line is followed by others overlapping in succession at set intervals and at specific pitches.

CANTATA: A multiple-movement work, usually for chorus, vocal soloists, and orchestra, with religious or secular text.

CHAMBER MUSIC: Compositions for a small group of players, usually between two and nine, best suited to intimate performance spaces.

CHORALE: A hymn, usually sung by a congregation or by a chorus in a sacred CANTATA or PASSION.

CHORUS: A vocal ensemble usually consisting of male and female voices (also called "mixed chorus"); the women sing the soprano and alto parts, the men sing the tenor and bass parts.

CODA: The closing passage of a composition or of a single movement within a multiple-movement composition.

COLOR: A descriptive term applied to music as a means of indicating the shading of tones made possible by dynamics (the range of volume from loud to soft) or phrasing (how the notes are articulated).

CONCERTO: A work for solo instrument (or instruments) and orchestra, usually with three movements.

CONCERTO GROSSO: A multiple-movement work that involves contrast and interplay between a small group of instruments and a larger orchestra.

CONDUCTOR: The person who leads a performance, setting the tempo and cueing musicians as needed, and also interprets the music by indicating how it is to be phrased.

CONTINUO: See BASSO CONTINUO.

COUNTERPOINT: A style of polyphony in which two or more independent melodic lines are sung or played simultaneously, yet are meshed in subtle ways that help to form a cohesive musical statement.

CRESCENDO: An indication music should get louder.

DA CAPO ARIA: Italian for "to the head." In Baroque opera and oratorio, it signifies a type of vocal solo that is in three sections. After the first and second sections are performed, the singer goes back to the beginning of the piece and repeats the first part, usually embellishing the vocal line (ORNAMENTATION) of the first section.

DECRESCENDO: An indication that the music should get softer.

DIMINUENDO: See DECRESCENDO.

FORTE: An indication that the music should be loud.

FORTISSIMO: An indication that the music should be very loud.

FUGUE: A polyphonic form of composition in which a theme, or "subject," is stated alone, then followed by another statement of the subject starting on a different pitch ("answer"), while the original melodic line continues with new material ("countersubject"). A third or fourth answer may enter as well. All of the material then undergoes thematic development.

GIGUE: A dance form, developed from the jig danced in the British Isles, usually placed at the end of a Baroque suite and played very fast.

GLISSANDO: A technique of sliding a finger across the keys of a piano or strings of a harp, resulting in a blur of notes.

HARMONY: The result of notes sounding simultaneously and producing chords that help to establish a sense of tonality—major or minor key, for example.

INCIDENTAL MUSIC: Music, usually in short movements, originally meant to be played at key points during a play or other stage work.

LARGO: A slow tempo.

LIED (plural: LIEDER): The German word for ART SONG.

MA NON TROPPO: A qualifying term applied to a tempo marking: Allegro, ma non troppo ("Fast, but not too fast").

MASS: A choral composition in multiple movements using texts of the Latin liturgical rite of the Roman Catholic Church.

MELODY: A sequence of notes or pitches that produces a coherent musical thought.

MEZZO-FORTE: An indication that the music should be moderately loud.

MEZZO-PIANO: An indication that the music should be moderately soft.

MINUET: A courtly dance in three-quarter time, a standard movement of a multiple-movement work of the seventeenth and eighteenth centuries, in which the opening and closing sections are essentially the same, with a contrasting section in between (see TRIO).

MOLTO: A term of emphasis placed in front of a tempo marking: Molto adagio ("very slow").

MONOPHONY: Music with a single melodic line without accompaniment.

MOVEMENT: A self-contained portion of composition with other such sections, as in a symphony, sonata, or concerto.

NOTATION: A system of writing music using symbols to indicate specific pitches (notes).

OP: Abbreviation for OPUS.

OPUS: From the Latin for "a work," the term is used in music to indicate a published work that is numbered chronologically in order of publication, not necessarily the date of composition. Example: Op. 7 indicates the seventh work by a composer to be published. Within a single opus number, there may be more than one independent piece. Example: Op. 15, no. 3 identifies the third piece in the composer's fifteenth published work.

ORATORIO: A large-scale work for solo voices, chorus, and orchestra with a narrative or contemplative text on a religious subject.

ORCHESTRA: An ensemble of musicians, usually consisting of several sections—strings, woodwinds, brass, and percussion.

ORNAMENTATION: The practice of adding to—embellishing—a printed musical line by a singer or instrumentalist.

OVERTURE: A single-movement orchestral work that precedes an opera or other stage work. Some overtures are written independently of anything else, meant to stand alone as a short concert piece (often called "concert overture").

PASSION: A large-scale work for vocal soloists, chorus, and orchestra based on texts from one of the four gospels of the New Testament dealing with the arrest, trial, death, and burial of Jesus.

PIANISSIMO: An indication that the music should be very soft.

PIZZICATO: A technique of playing a string instrument by plucking on the strings with the finger instead of sliding a bow across them.

POLYPHONY: Music with two or more independent melodic lines that intersect and interact in a coherent fashion.

PRELUDE: 1) A composition that serves to introduce an opera or a Baroque instrumental suite; 2) a short work, usually for keyboard and in a variety of forms, that may be paired with a fugue in the same key, or intended as a stand-alone composition.

PRESTO: A very fast tempo.

QUODLIBET: A composition, especially associated with the Baroque era, that combines two or more popular melodies simultaneously.

RECITAL: A performance for a single instrumentalist, or an instrumentalist or vocalist with an accompanist.

RECITATIVE: Solo vocal music in a free-form style, accompanied by keyboard or other instruments, that introduces or separates arias and other formal sections of an oratorio, cantata, or opera.

REQUIEM: A choral composition in multiple movements using texts from the Latin Mass for the Dead.

RITARDANDO: A direction to slow down the tempo.

RONDO: An instrumental work in which the opening section returns several times, separated in each case by different, contrasting material.

RUBATO: An indication to stretch out a musical line slightly, to make it a little less strict in rhythm.

SARABANDE: A slow, stately dance form commonly included in a Baroque instrumental suite.

SCHERZO: Literally "joke" in Italian, this term describes a fast-paced movement within a symphony, sonata, string quartet, etc., that replaced the minuet; it typically begins and ends with the same material and has a contrasting section in between (see TRIO).

SONATA: A work, usually containing multiple movements, for solo instrument or solo instrument with keyboard accompaniment.

SONATA FORM: A musical structure consisting of three main sections—an exposition of two or more contrasting themes; a development of one or more of those themes; and a recapitulation of the exposition material, which may be modified in various ways.

SUITE: 1) An instrumental piece, particularly associated with the Baroque era, but also occurring in the Classical era, consisting of several dance forms; 2) any instrumental work containing excerpts from an opera or ballet, or independent movements that do not conform to a symphony and may or may not be related by mood or other characteristics.

SYMPHONIC POEM: See TONE POEM.

SYMPHONY: A large-scale work, usually with four movements, for orchestra.

TEMPO: The speed of a composition.

TEXTURE: The aural effect produced by a combination of sounds from an instrumental ensemble, from light and transparent to dark and heavy.

THEME: A melody.

THEME AND VARIATIONS: A composition that begins with the statement of a theme, followed by a series of separate melodic, harmonic, and/or rhythmic variations on it.

TONE POEM: A descriptive or suggestive composition for orchestra based on a nonmusical idea—a work of literature, an element of nature, an incident in history, etc. Also called "symphonic poem."

TRANSCRIPTION: An arrangement of a work, usually done by someone other than the original composer and usually involving a substantial change in instrumentation.

TRIO: 1) A chamber-music work for three instruments; 2) the middle portion of a MINUET or SCHERZO.

TWELVE-TONE MUSIC: A complex style of music, also called "seri-alism," developed in the early-twentieth century by Arnold Schoenberg, in which all melodic and harmonic material is generated from a predetermined sequence ("tone row") of all twelve notes in the common Western scale.

VIVACE: A very fast tempo.

Resources for Curious Listeners

Needless to say, listening to performances provides the greatest education in classical music. In the case of live concerts, in addition to what you get to hear, you'll usually find background on the composers and their works in the program books handed out at the door.

Beyond ears-on experiences, there are various and valuable resources, from the printed word to the cyber word, that can help the Curious Listener become an informed one.

Books

For reading up on the subject, local libraries are a good (and certainly economical) place to start; well-stocked bookstores also can be counted on to have some useful material about music and musicians. Many books, written primarily for formal students of music and practicing scholars, can be a little intimidating, but a variety of general-information guidebooks are available for novice listeners, too. There are biographies of numerous composers from centuries ago to today; many leading performers, particularly from the last hundred years or so, have prompted life studies as well.

Here are some suggestions for reading material that should make delving into classical music easy and fruitful.

The Billboard Illustrated History of Classical Music, edited by Stanley Sadie: For a single reference book, this one has much to recommend it, not the least of which is the steady editing hand of Stanley Sadie, who provided the leadership for *The New Grove Dictionary of Music and Musicians* (see below). The book covers the history, styles, personalities, and instruments of music, complemented by some nine hundred illustrations.

Classical Music: An Introduction to Classical Music Through the Great Composers and Their Works, John Stanley: This richly illustrated coffee-table book makes an excellent companion for those testing the classical waters. Neatly arranged chronologically, with many a stop on the side to look at certain topics in detail, the book presents music in its historical context.

Classical Music: The 50 Greatest Composers and Their 1,000 Greatest Works, Phil G. Goulding: Here's a very extensive guide written specifically with the beginning listener in mind. There are very readable biographies, each one capped by three lists of compositions worth hearing—"a starter kit," "a top ten," and "a master collection." Entries also cover the history and fundamentals of music.

An Encyclopedia of Classical Music, edited by Robert Ainsley: Another well-illustrated guide that provides fairly extensive information on how music works, not just who has written and performed it. This extra material on the mechanics of making music—harmony, dynamics, tempo, etc.—may go over some heads, but there still is a lot here for the newcomer to absorb easily.

The Lives of the Great Composers, **Third Edition,** Harold C. Schonberg: Schonberg, former chief music critic of the *New York Times,* provides one of the most reader-friendly books written about classical composers. The biographical material is thorough and fascinating, the critical judgments fair and thoroughly persuasive.

The New Grove Dictionary of Music and Musicians, **Second Edition,** edited by Stanley Sadie: This is the mother of all musical dictionaries, with 29 volumes, 29,000 articles, and 25 million words. Although it's geared more to the advanced music lover, the *Grove* need not intimidate the freshly curious. The wealth and breadth of material is astonishing, covering composers, performers, and instruments from virtually every corner of the globe, as well as such heady issues as feminism, Marxism, and postmodernism in music. It's awfully hard to just read one entry in the *Grove;* there seems to be a fascinating topic on every page.

Although the price of the dictionary (original list price $4,850) will keep it out of the average home, it is available at many libraries. There is also an Internet option. Daily, monthly, and annual rates are available for access to the complete *Grove* online. The Website, which includes graphics (some in 3-D) and aural links, is: www.grovemusic.com.

The NPR Classical Music Companion: Terms and Concepts from A to Z,
Miles Hoffman: This highly informative but never pedantic
guide explains some of the most important elements of classical
music. Hoffman will be familiar to listeners of NPR's *Perfor-mance Today,* for which he contributes the engaging feature
"Coming to Terms."

The NPR Guide to Building a Classical CD Collection, Second Edition, Ted
Libbey: First, this very readable book offers a well-thought-out
compendium of recommended recordings, covering orchestral
music, concertos, chamber music, solo keyboard music, sacred
and choral music, and opera. But Libbey, who offers the most
popular segment on NPR's *Performance Today,* "The PT Basic
Record Library," has written much more than a consumer
guide. He provides a great deal of information about the com-posers and compositions themselves.

The Oxford Dictionary of Music, Second Edition, Michael Kennedy:
This handy, first-rate, one-volume encyclopedia put together by
a leading British critic crams in more than eleven thousand
entries on performers, works, instruments, and musical terms.

The Virtuosi: Classical Music's Great Performers from Paganini to Pava-rotti, Harold C. Schonberg: For succinct, entertaining, and very
informative biographical sketches of classical stars, this volume
cannot be bettered. The book was also published under the title
The Glorious Ones.

Magazines

Once upon a time, classical music magazines were, if not
plentiful, then at least noticeable. Over the years, such special-

ized periodicals, from *The Etude* to *Musical America*, have pretty much faded away. While it is possible to find several magazines devoted exclusively to opera, finding one about classical music in general is another matter. The closest thing would be publications devoted primarily to reviewing new (or reissued) classical recordings.

BBC Music Magazine: Probably the most useful periodical for newcomers to classical music, it provides a good deal more than record reviews. There are articles on music itself, as well as musicians. Each issue also comes with a CD and an informative article about the works contained on it.

Gramophone Magazine: Like *BBC Music Magazine*, this publication is from England. It has for many decades been valued for its opinions about the latest classical recordings. Articles on works of music, the recording industry, and leading performers are also regularly featured.

Websites

If you do a search for "classical music" on the web, thousands of sites will be listed; it would take months to get through all of them. But this avenue certainly has the potential to satisfy Curious Listeners seeking information on various musical topics, concerts, recordings, etc. Here are three that might make good jumping-off spots for cyber-traveling. (Needless to say, Websites have a way of coming and going without notice. If these disappear, just keep searching. There will be others.)

andante.com: This large, ambitious site offers quite a treasure of resource materials, including discographies of performers, notes on dozens of compositions, a listing of recordings in print, and, above all, access to *The Concise Grove Dictionary of Music.*

classicalworks.com: This site also offers a thoughtful, easily navigated presentation of basic information on music and musicians.

essentialsofmusic.com: Although it's run by the Sony Classical record label, this user-friendly site is not a giant commercial. There are well-organized pages devoted to the history of classical music, composer biographies, and more.

Video

There are assorted performances on tape featuring artists from the past and today, but these generally offer no more in content than what can be heard on audio recordings. For something of an educational nature, there is, however, one prime product. You don't have to be a kid to get information and enjoyment from the acclaimed series of programs that started in 1958 and ran for several years: *Leonard Bernstein's Young People's Concerts* (Kultur Films, Inc.), which the conductor gave with the New York Philharmonic. A complete set of the TV broadcasts is available on video, as well as sampler sets and a few individual tapes, including "What is Classical Music?" "What Does Music Mean?" and "What Makes Music Symphonic?"

Index